Cognitive-Behavioral Therapy for Anxious Children: Therapist Manual

third edition

Coping Cat

Philip C. Kendall, Ph.D., ABPP
&
Kristina A. Hedtke, M.A.

Temple University
Child and Adolescent Anxiety Disorders Clinic

Workbook Publishing offers evidence-based child and adolescent workbooks, treatment manuals, and training materials.

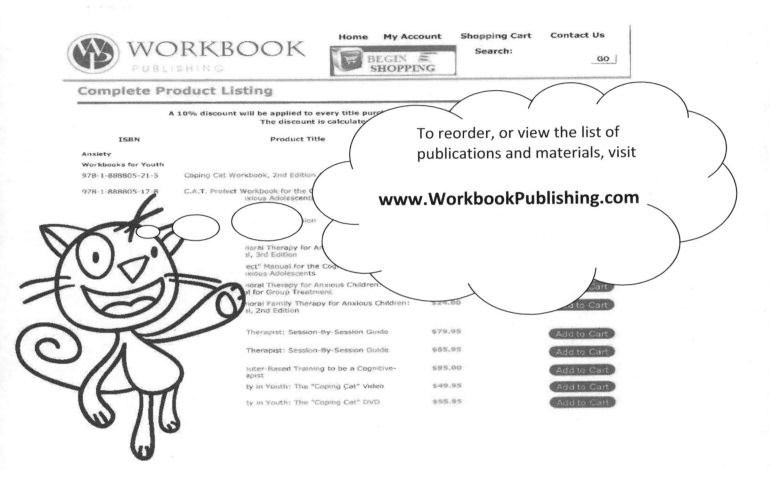

Available are

- DVDs for training in the provision of the intervention programs and treatments.
- An interactive computer-assisted program (*Camp Cope-A-Lot*) to address anxiety in youth.
- Materials for youth with depression, anger management issues, and impulsivity.
- Materials for *EMOTION*, a group program for both anxiety and depression, that has compatible materials for working with parents.
- Materials for anxiety in youth, including child anxiety (*Coping cat program*; *Brief Coping cat program*) and anxiety in adolescents (*C.A.T. Project*).

Cognitive-Behavioral Therapy for Anxious Children: Therapist Manual

third edition

Coping Cat

Philip C. Kendall, Ph.D., ABPP
&
Kristina A. Hedtke, M.A.

Temple University
Child and Adolescent Anxiety Disorders Clinic

Cognitive-Behavioral Therapy for Anxious Children: Therapist Manual
Third Edition

Copyright © 2006
by Workbook Publishing

ISBN-13: 978-1-888805-22-2
ISBN-10: 1-888805-22-6

This manual benefited greatly from the input of numerous colleagues and clients. Special thanks to all trainees and professionals who have studied and worked within the Child and Adolescent Anxiety Disorders Clinic (CAADC). Also, the input of the many youth and their families who have participated in activities within the CAADC is very much appreciated.

Printed in the United Stated of America

Workbook Publishing
P.O. Box 67
Ardmore, PA 19003-0067 USA
www.workbookpublishing.com

Precis and Acknowledgements

This therapist manual has three sections. In the first, the program is introduced in an overview fashion, with a discussion of the implementation of manual-based treatment with clinical flexibility. The second section contains detailed descriptions of the specific treatment sessions. A series of notes, or tips, from experienced therapists (referred to as "Tips from the Trenches") are appended to each of the treatment sessions in the form of a bullet-list with the main idea of each tip printed in bold. Based on research and clinical input, section three provides therapist resources for dealing with comorbid concerns and addressing complicating factors that may impact treatment success (e.g., family difficulties).

This therapist manual could not have been completed without the input and cooperation of numerous therapists and diagnosticians. These individuals include my coauthors on the first edition, Drs. Martha Kane, Bonnie Howard, and Lynne Siqueland, who were invaluable in assisting in the initial organization of the manual, and the many other collaborators who have had input into the procedures now described herein: Drs. Anne Marie Albano, Erika Brady, Tamar Chansky, Muniya Choudhury, Brian Chu, Ellen Flannery-Schroeder, Elizabeth Gosch, Aude Henin, Jennifer Hudson, Elizabeth Kortlander, Amy Krain, Jennefer Panas MacDonald, Abbe Marrs-Garcia, Suzie Panichelli-Mindel, Sandra Pimentel, Kevin Ronan, Fran Sessa, Michael Southam-Gerow, Cynthia Suveg, Kim Treadwell, Melissa Warman, and Alicia Webb. These therapists and others (i.e. Aleta Angelosante, Lindsey Bergman, Jonathan Comer, Alicia Hughes, Jennifer Jones, Joanna Robin, and Timothy Verduin) provided suggestions for the "Tips from the Trenches" that are provided at the end of each session. Other CBT therapists, such as those participating in the CAMS multi-site evaluation of treatments for anxiety disorders in youth, my international colleagues working on translated versions of the treatment manuals and materials, and those who have interacted with me during conferences and workshops, are also thanked for their suggestions and interest. Special thanks to the numerous graduate students who also help to keep the manual alive, and who will soon rise to the list of doctoral colleagues (above). Kristi Hedtke, my coauthor on this second edition, is singled out for her energetic efforts to improve the information in both the workbook and this therapist manual. Collectively, all are thanked, by me and by Kristi, as is anyone whom we may have inadvertently omitted. Finally, appreciation is expressed to the many anxious children and their parents who have participated in the program over the years.

The development of this treatment program and its research evaluation have gone hand in hand. Preparation of this work was facilitated by and evaluated within several research grants from the National Institute of Mental Health (e.g., MH60653; MH59087; MH64484; MH63747).

Introduction
Cognitive-Behavioral Therapy for Anxious Children

This treatment manual describes a 16-session program for the treatment of anxiety disorders, specifically generalized anxiety disorder, social phobia, and separation anxiety disorder, in children and young adolescents.[1] The overall approach is cognitive-behavioral; an integration of the demonstrated efficacies of the behavioral approach (e.g., exposure tasks, relaxation training, role play activities, practice and reward) with an added emphasis of the cognitive information-processing factors associated with each individual's anxieties (emotional distress, anticipatory dread). Social forces (e.g., peers, families) are also included, as are emotion understanding and emotion management skills. The approach represents a rational amalgam.

The overall goal is to teach children to recognize signs of unwanted anxious arousal and to let these signs serve as cues for the use of anxiety management strategies. Identifying the cognitive processes associated with excessive anxious arousal, training in cognitive strategies for anxiety management, training in behavioral relaxation, and performance-based practice opportunities are sequenced within the manual to build skill upon skill. The greatest emphasis within the treatment program is placed upon the following general strategies:

- ➢ graduated sequence of training tasks and assignments
- ➢ role play procedures
- ➢ coping modeling
- ➢ homework assignments ("Show-That-I-Can"—STIC tasks)
- ➢ affective education
- ➢ awareness of bodily reactions when anxious
- ➢ relaxation training
- ➢ identification and modification of anxious self-talk
- ➢ contingent rewards
- ➢ practice of newly acquired skills in increasingly anxiety-provoking situations (i.e., exposure tasks), both imaginal and in-vivo
- ➢ design and completion of a "child-developed" commercial

The strategies described herein are specifically coordinated with the first (Kendall, 2000) and second editions of the *Coping cat workbook* (Kendall & Hedtke, 2006), a client workbook that contains exercises and tasks consistent with the information presented and discussed in the treatment. The two go hand-in-hand, and are meant to be used together.

---

[1] Although the manual is appropriate for young adolescents, the word "child" will be used in referring to the client. Readers interested in treating older adolescents are referred to the C.A.T. Project Manual (Kendall, Choudhury, Hudson, & Webb, 2002; www.WorkbookPublishing.com). Also, to increase the readability, the pronoun "he" will be used instead of "he/she" (himself/herself) to refer to the client and "she" to refer to the therapist.

The 16-session program is divided into two parts. The first eight sessions are the training segment and the second eight sessions are the practice (exposure tasks) segment. In addition, two sessions between the therapist and the parent(s) (or one or more of the child's guardians) are scheduled at session 4 and session 9. The theory that guides the treatment is described in Kendall (1993; 2006). For those interested in working within a family therapy context, see the therapist manual for family therapy for anxious children (Howard, Chu, Krain, Marrs-Garcia, & Kendall, 2000; Howard & Kendall, 1996; see also Fauber & Kendall, 1992). For those who wish to work in groups, see the therapist manual for group treatment (Flannery-Schroeder & Kendall, 1996). For more information about therapist manuals and treatment materials, consult the web (www.WorkbookPublishing.com).

Throughout the treatment, concepts and skills are introduced in a sequential order from most basic to more difficult. The therapist functions as a coping model as all new skills are introduced—demonstrating not only the skill for the child, but also the difficulties that might be experienced and the strategies to overcome the difficulties. The therapist demonstrates first in each new situation. The child is invited to participate with the therapist in role plays, using a "tag-along" procedure (see Ollendick & Cerny, 1981). Finally, the child is encouraged to role play scenes alone, practicing newly acquired skills. Within each session and throughout the training program, the level of anxiety is gradually increased, beginning with the non-stressful situations and gradually incorporating increasing levels of anxiety. "Show-That-I-Can" (STIC) tasks are assigned as tasks to be completed outside of the therapy setting to help show the applicability of what has been addressed during the session.

Several important concepts are sequentially introduced to the child during the training segment of the program, beginning with the awareness of bodily reactions to feelings and developing a recognition of those reactions that are specific to anxiety (coordinated with client assignments in the *Coping cat workbook*). The child is trained to use physical reactions as a cue to the presence of anxiety. Anxious children lack skills associated with understanding their ability to modify their emotions (Southam-Gerow & Kendall, 2000), so these limitations are addressed in treatment. The next general concept that is introduced to the child is learning to recognize and modify his anxious "self-talk" (see Kendall & MacDonald, 1993; Ronan, Kendall & Rowe, 1994; Treadwell & Kendall, 1996). Both his expectations and fears about what will happen and the role he sees for himself in the situation are important. The third concept presented to the child is the modification of his anxious self-talk into coping self-talk and developing plans for coping with his anxieties more effectively in different situations. The fourth concept introduced to the child is self-rating and reward, even for partial success.

These four concepts are summarized in a 4-step plan for coping with anxiety. To help facilitate the child's recall of the plan, an acronym will be introduced. The acronym forms the FEAR plan, with each letter of FEAR standing for a step in the plan:

Feeling **F**rightened?
Expecting bad things to happen?
Attitudes and **A**ctions that can help
Results and **R**ewards

The second segment of the program is devoted to the application and practice of the newly acquired knowledge and skills in increasingly anxiety provoking situations. The same training strategies are employed, including coping modeling, role play activities, and STIC assignments. The situations that are presented to each child are individually designed for him based on his own particular fears and worries (as assessed during initial sessions and again during Session 8; see also Kendall et al., 2005a). The first practice sessions involve imaginal, in-office exposure, associated with low levels of anxiety and are followed by actual, in-vivo experiences in low stress situations. Subsequent sessions involve repeating this process in situations that are even more stressful for the child, helping the child to master his skills by exposing him to a number of different anxiety-provoking situations. Finally, the last session includes videotaping of a "commercial" about learning to cope with anxiety—giving the child an opportunity to share and show off what he has learned with others.

It is worth noting that this treatment has been evaluated in several randomized clinical trials with one-year follow-up data conducted both in the United States (e.g., Kendall, 1994; Kendall et al., 1997) and in Australia (e.g., Barrett, Dadds & Rapee, 1996). The outcomes have been favorable; with 3.35 year-follow-up of one study (Kendall & Southam-Gerow, 1996) and 7.4 year-year follow-up of the second study (Kendall, Safford, Flannery-Schroeder, & Webb, 2004) providing evidence of the maintenance of gains. In conjunction with the criteria recommended for use in determination of treatments that qualify as having been supported by empirical research (Chambless & Hollon, 1998), reviewers of the literature indicate that the treatment is empirically-supported (see Kazdin & Weisz, 1998; Ollendick & King, 1998; Ollendick, King, & Chorpita, 2006).

Discussion of a broad range of topics related to the treatment of anxious youth is presented in Kendall and Holmbeck (1991); Kendall, Hudson, Choudhury, Webb, and Pimentel (2005b); and Kendall and Treadwell (1996). Issues related to the transportability of the treatment from the research setting to the service clinic appears in Kendall and Southam-Gerow (1995) and Hudson, Krain, and Kendall (2001). Evidence regarding the applicability of the treatment across changing diagnostic criteria appears in Kendall and Warman (1996) and across ethnicity and gender appears in Treadwell, Flannery, and Kendall (1995). Readers interested in additional data with regard to the treatment are encouraged to consult the following sources: Regarding process variables, see Chu and Kendall (2004) and Creed and Kendall (2005); regarding maternal expectations and attributions about coping in anxious youth, see Kortlander, Kendall, and Panichelli-Mindel (1997); regarding the social expectations and self-perceptions of anxious youth, see Chansky and Kendall (1997). For suggestions and specific considerations of strategies related to the exposure tasks, see Kendall, Robin, Hedtke, Gosch, Flannery-Schroeder, and Suveg, (2005a). A description of the Child and Adolescent Anxiety Disorders Clinic and its services can be found online (www.childanxiety.org) and appears in Kendall et al. (2005b). Examples of case applications can be found in Suveg, Comer, Furr, and Kendall (2006) and Krain, Hudson, Coles, and Kendall (2002), and discussions of developmental, familial, and related topics can be found in the Special Issue of the *International Journal of Cognitive Psychotherapy* (2006) and in the Special Issue of *Cognitive and Behavioral Practice* (vol. 11, 2004).

Flexibility within Fidelity

Treatment manuals should be guiding templates, not rigid cookbooks. In the pages that follow, we have organized and sequenced the strategies described in the introduction to help youth manage and overcome anxious distress. The approach is structured, but good clinical skills and therapist flexibility are needed to individualize the program for each child's specific needs—to maximize gains.

Therapists working within manual-based treatment programs are referred to an article entitled "Breathing life into a manual" which provides discussion of several ways to be manual-based and flexible in the provision of treatment services (Kendall, Chu, Gifford, Hayes, & Nauta, 1999). Therapists are not only exposed to the strategies of a specified intervention program, but also make necessary adjustments to have the program be a "good fit" for each child and his family. Therapy certainly benefits from therapist sensitivity to (a) comorbid conditions, (b) developmental level, (c) familial and environmental stressors, (d) socioeconomic status, and (e) home and school functioning.

With knowledge of such individual differences, the following treatment program is applied flexibly, but within fidelity--modifying cognitive and/or behavioral components of the treatment to best help the particular child. In other words, the therapist focuses on the purpose and goals of the session and modifies the tasks/activities to fit the needs of each individual child.

To encourage therapists to apply the treatment flexibly, but within fidelity, we have added a new feature to the third edition of the *Coping cat* treatment manual. Embedded within the session content, "call-outs," such as the one presented below point to activities or content that can be modified to flexibly meet a child's needs.

Although all session activities described in the manual (not just the ones that are tagged) can be implemented flexibly, our hope is that the "F L E X" call-out will (a) serve as a reminder for therapists to remain flexible when presenting treatment content and (b) help therapists select an activity or content that lends itself easily to flexible use. In addition to the call-out, we also include suggestions from actual therapists, listed herein as "Tips from the Trenches." These, too, are intended to be flexible and helpful suggestions from those who have passed through these doors before you.

The following pages contain session-by-session descriptions that detail the features of the treatment. In each instance a statement of the overall purpose of the session is presented followed by an outline of the specific goals and tasks. Although not intended as a transcript of the treatment, the manual was designed to serve as a guiding template for the integration and application of the treatment strategies for the treatment of youth anxiety.

Table of Contents

Table of Contents Cont.

Building Rapport and Treatment Orientation
Session 1

Purpose

Get to know one another and explain basic information about the treatment. Begin to gather information about situations that make the child anxious and the child's reactions to signs and feelings of anxiety.

Goals

1. Build rapport
2. Orient child to the program
3. Encourage/support the child's participation
4. Assign an initial simple Show-That-I-Can (STIC) task
5. Engage in fun end-of-session activity

Tasks

1.   <u>Build rapport</u>

It is essential that the therapy not move too quickly, because anxious children are often avoidant, generally fearful or wary, and typically not familiar with our inquiries about their feelings, thinking, or self-talk. Rapport between the anxious child and the therapist is critical to the success of the therapy, and it is certainly worthwhile to devote ample time to the establishment of a trusting relationship between the child and therapist.

> ➤ Opening conversation
>
> The first 10-15 minutes are for opening conversation: no focus, no threat. The therapist asks the child to make himself at home, look around the room, try any of the toys or games he'd like, and encourages the child to suggest a fun activity for the end of the hour/session. The therapist has suggestions of possible activities if the child has difficulty naming one. When the child has become somewhat involved and has selected an activity for the end of the session, the therapist can then agree in a manner something like the following: "Ok, that would be fun to do. Let's be sure to save 10 minutes to do that together." The therapist checks a watch and notes the time. Trust is built on reliable recall of the "deal" and sticking to it.

> ➤ Get to know each other   **FLEX**
>
> To introduce the therapist's need to gather information, and the idea that this information is important to the therapist, play a "Personal Facts" game (you can use pp. 1-2 in the *Coping cat workbook* as a guide). In this game both the child and therapist supply answers to the same questions, such as "What is your middle name?" "How old are you?" "How many brothers and sisters do you have?" etc. In addition, including questions about favorite TV shows, videogames, music, heroes, and superheroes can provide information that will be helpful later in the treatment. After giving answers, the therapist and child playfully quiz each other on the answers, with a small prize going to the players (i.e., provide a reward for participating in question answering). It is important that the therapist recall the information

accurately, as this information is one of the child's first attempts to share personal data with the therapist. It is suggested that the therapist be comfortable with the child's asking personal information and with providing answers to appropriate questions.

2. **Orient child to the program**

➤ Give a brief overview of the program (e.g., meeting each week) and create the sense that this program is a joint effort between the therapist and child.

➤ Provide a review of the reasons for the program ("Helps some kids with…").

➤ Mention the goals for treatment, including being able to identify anxious feelings, recognize anxious thoughts, and use appropriate coping strategies. These ideas are introduced as "knowing when you're anxious" and "knowing what to do about it"—with the focus of the first few sessions on "knowing when you're anxious," followed by sessions that will focus on "knowing what to do about it."

3. **Encourage/support the child's participation**

➤ Invite the child's questions about the treatment and re-open the invitation periodically until the child begins to share his questions and concerns.

➤ Stress to the child that information from his point of view is very important. Ask the child to tell some stories of fun activities, family trips, or school events that were particularly enjoyable. Reward participation, encourage verbalization, and ask easy-to-answer questions.

➤ Point out that different people see things differently (Provide concrete examples such as "A brick wall that is very tall to a child may be small to a full-grown and tall man." "A tasty treat for one person may be the cause of an upset stomach for someone else."). Emphasize that we're interested in "What *you* see and think about various situations."

4. **Assign an initial simple Show-That-I-Can (STIC) task**

➤ To introduce out-of-session activities, the child is told that Show-That-I-Can (STIC) tasks are assigned and reviewed at each meeting. For the first STIC task, give the child the *Coping cat workbook* and ask him (a) to bring the workbook to the next session and (b) to write in it a brief example of a time when he feels really great—not upset or worried. The child is asked to focus on what made him comfortable and what he thought at that time. To help the child understand the assignment, the therapist provides an example of a time when she felt really great and describes what she thought. Then the child is given a chance to do the same.

➤ The child is told that he can earn 2 points (or stickers for younger children) at the next meeting to be entered in the "bank" on page 72 of the *Coping cat workbook* for having completed the STIC task. The points earned are used to purchase rewards periodically during the program (after Sessions 4, 8, 12, and 16). The child can select the rewards he wants to earn and enter them in the "reward menu" on page 73 of the *Coping cat workbook*. Options for rewards after Sessions 4 and 8 can be small toys, books, or games. The rewards available after Sessions 12 and 16 are social rewards such as time spent playing a computer game with the therapist or going out for ice cream.

5. <u>**Engage in fun end-of-session activity**</u>

➤ After the session content has been addressed, take 5-10 minutes to play a game or engage in an activity (e.g., looking up something on the internet, telling funny stories, talking about episodes of favorite T.V. shows) that was selected with the child at the beginning of the session. Engaging in a fun activity serves several purposes. Foremost, it's fun! When a child views therapy as a potentially fun and a positive experience, he will be more likely to want to attend subsequent sessions and engage in session activities. Also, engaging in the fun activity that had been selected at the start of the session shows the child that that the therapist "follows-through:" helping to establish trust. Finally, playing a game or engaging in a fun activity at the end of session is a reward for the child's attendance and effort in the session.

Tips from the Trenches

Session 1

> To help therapists browse the tips with ease, the main idea/topic of each tip has been bolded. This formatting applies to each session's "Tips from the Trenches."

➤ As a therapist, **try to make the first session fun!** Playing a game at the beginning and/or end of the session and giving the child a "tour" of the clinic can help ease the child's fears about commencing treatment.

➤ **Proceed slowly** because the therapy situation alone is one that provokes anxiety, and the therapist often becomes another person that the child feels he has to please.

➤ It is useful for the therapist to **have knowledge of the child's interests** (i.e., likes and dislikes) prior to the first session. Knowing a little bit about the child shows the child that the therapist is interested in getting to know him.

➤ The therapist can begin to **normalize the child's anxiety** by reviewing that anxiety is a normal reaction and that anxiety problems are common among kids. The therapist can discuss how many children go the child's school and how likely it is that other children in the child's class have problems with anxiety.

➤ It is important that the therapist **acknowledge, listen to, and respond to the child's concerns** about being in treatment and how the decision was made.

➤ **When resistance or anger is noted,** it may be helpful for the therapist to ask the child "Are there any things that you can think of that would make coming here more fun?" The child can also be given several days to think about being part of treatment. The therapist's position is that she does not want to force the child to change or insist on participation if there are no problems. Instead, the therapist offers herself as someone who might be able to help the child with some things that don't seem to go as well as the child would like.

➤ **The therapist describes her role to the child as being the child's "coach."** That is, like a coach or a tutor for the child who wants to improve in a skill or learn how to accomplish something that's challenging, the therapist provides structure and helpful hints.

- ➤ It is emphasized that **the therapist and child work as a "team"**—the therapist has some suggestions to offer and the child knows himself best.
- ➤ It may be helpful, especially for younger children, if **the therapist invites the parent(s) to join the session** to review logistics, discuss confidentiality, schedule the next session, and provide a very brief overview of treatment.
- ➤ **The therapist reviews confidentiality** and the limits of confidentiality with both the parent(s) and child. As a team, the therapist discusses with the parent(s) and child which aspects of the child's treatment and which aspects of the sessions will be shared with the parent(s). Discussing confidentiality during the first session reduces the possibility of a misunderstanding later in treatment.
- ➤ **The importance of weekly attendance is emphasized** for the parent(s). Should the child need to miss a session, a phone call at least 24 hours in advance is expected. However, the parent(s) should be informed that it is important for the child to attend each week to achieve the best treatment results.

Identifying Anxious Feelings
Session 2

Purpose

Review briefly the goals of the treatment. Help the child identify different types of feelings and to distinguish anxious/worried feelings from other types of feelings. Normalize feelings of fear and anxiety. Have the child begin to identify his own specific somatic responses to anxiety. Begin to develop a hierarchy of anxiety-provoking situations.

Goals

1. Build rapport
2. Review STIC task from Session 1
3. Introduce the concept that different feelings have different physical expressions
4. Normalize the experience of fears and anxiety
5. Begin to construct a hierarchy of anxiety-provoking situations
6. Assign STIC task

Tasks

1. **Build rapport**
   - If the child needs to settle down or ask questions, or if additional time needs to be spent on building rapport, a brief game is played or a fun activity is shared with the child.

2. **Review STIC task from Session 1**
   - Discuss the feeling-great situation that the child experienced during the intervening days and recorded in the *Coping cat workbook*, particularly focusing on the different pleasurable aspects. The therapist asks how the child felt, what the child thought about, and how the child acted. It is unlikely that the child will be able to fully describe such a situation. This limitation, however, can be noted as it may be informative about which aspects of the therapeutic program will need more or less attention and effort. Reward points or give stickers for effort--even modest participation (shaping).
   - If the child did not complete the STIC task from Session 1, the therapist is not punitive, but (a) spends time at the start of the session to complete the task and (b) explores why the child was unable to complete the task (e.g., child did not understand assignment, child forgot to complete assignment). The therapist asks the child to think back over the week and to talk about his experiences with the therapist's probing. For any session that the child does not complete the previous week's STIC task, the therapist and child begin by completing the STIC task in session.

3. **Introduce the concept that different feelings have different physical expressions**
   - Discuss different feelings

     Discuss the idea that people's bodies can do different things in response to different feelings, and that different facial expressions and postures are clues to their feelings. The therapist can have the child list as many feelings as he can think of in the *Coping cat workbook* (p.5), and try to assess which feelings the child is most comfortable talking about.

➤ Differentiate and label feelings

Use pictures of people showing different expressions (e.g., from magazines or in *Coping cat workbook, pp.* 6 and 8), both facial and entire body, that reflect different emotions and discuss what type of feeling each person might be experiencing (anxious expressions are included but the pictures are not limited to anxiety).

Begin to create a "Feelings Dictionary" by cutting out from magazines pictures that display physical responses of emotions, mounting them on butcher paper, and labeling the corresponding emotions below the picture. The therapist can post or display the work in the clinic for others to see (no identifying information such as initials or names). Alternatively, the child can take the project home to show his family.

➤ Role-play feelings

Introduce the idea of role play to the child. Role play with the child, acting out several different types of physically expressed emotions, taking turns guessing the emotion. It can be called "Feelings Charades." The therapist is alert for any difficulties the child is having differentiating and labeling emotions, and spends additional time on this element of the treatment if it is necessary. It is, for example, not uncommon for an anxious child to have trouble differentiating anxious feelings and angry ones or worried feelings and depressive ones.

4. **Normalize the experience of fears and anxiety**

➤ Initiate a discussion to reassure the child that all people have fears and anxieties (including adults who are admired as brave or labeled as heroes) and that the purpose of this program is to help him learn to recognize distress and cope with it effectively. We ALL feel anxious at various times, but some of us are better than others at knowing what to do when it happens. Some of us are better at "regulating" the emotion, like adjusting the volume on the radio. The skills to deal with anxiety can be learned. The

9

purpose of the program is to help the child learn and use the skills to manage anxious feelings.

➤ The therapist provides a coping model, disclosing a prior fear or situation which made her feel anxious. How it felt, how it was uncomfortable at first, and how it was handled are included in the disclosure.

➤ Using a real-life hero or a fantasy superhero the child has identified, the therapist and child can make up a story together about how this figure felt anxious but coped with this worry and overcame the challenge.

➤ Show the child the "No Fear" symbol (Allow the child to modify, expand, or replace this with a symbol of his own choosing). Explain the symbol: It's not that we expect to eliminate all fear, but that we will be able to manage it and cope with it. If the child finds it useful, keep the symbol plainly displayed in the office and use it on materials related to his participation in the program.

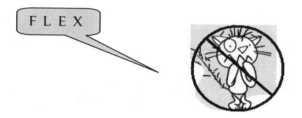

5. **Begin to construct a hierarchy of anxiety-provoking situations**

➤ Discuss anxious situations

Begin to discuss the specifics of the child's anxieties, including the types of situations that provoke anxiety, the child's reactions to anxiety (somatic and cognitive), and the child's response in the anxiety-provoking situations.

If the child finds it difficult to be specific about his anxieties, the therapist can use a procedure, recommended by Ollendick and Cerny (1981), in which the child tries to imagine an actual situation while the therapist observes his behavior for signs of anxiety. To introduce the procedure, the therapist models the process by imagining herself in an anxiety-provoking situation while describing each step. The child can then be invited to tag-along as the therapist repeats the imagining process with another situation and, finally, to imagine himself in an anxiety-provoking situation—with the therapist providing prompts as needed. Although the therapist can be encouraging by use of sights, sounds, and pictures, children will differ in their response to the use of imaginal exposure.

➤ Introduce the Feelings Thermometer (Subject Units of Distress Scale [SUDS])

The thermometer uses a scale ranging from 0-8:

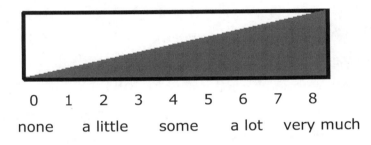

```
0   1   2   3   4   5   6   7   8
none   a little   some   a lot   very much
```

This scale can be used to help determine which situations are more anxiety provoking for the child. The therapist asks the question: "How much anxiety do you feel when _____?" "Give it a number."

FLEX

➤ Begin to construct a hierarchy
From the data collected thus far, the therapist and child begin to construct a brief hierarchy of the situations that seem to provoke anxiety in the child. To record this information, the therapist and child use either the situation cards found on pages 74-76 of the *Coping cat workbook* or the "fear ladder" found on page 77 of the *Coping cat workbook*. The decision as to which method to use can be made collaboratively. For young children, categorizing fears into "easy," "medium," and "challenging" may be a more simplistic and understandable procedure than building an actual hierarchy using the fear ladder. Regardless of the method chosen to document the child's fears (situation cards or fear ladder), the therapist takes note of which aspects of the different situations seem to be particularly easy and troublesome for the child. Be as specific as possible regarding the situations. For example, vague language is not preferred (e.g., "going to school"). Instead, enter specific

situations such as "taking a math test at school" or "eating in the cafeteria." Encourage the child to add to the cards/ladder whenever he remembers situations in which he feels anxious. It needn't be perfect at this juncture: the information will be reviewed and elaborated on during Session 8, and will then be used during the second half of the treatment when practice in using the coping skills is individualized for each child.

6. **Assign STIC task**

➢ Remind the child about the STIC task and review the idea of using the *Coping cat workbook* he was given in Session 1 as a journal to record his experiences. Or, if needed, the events can be tape recorded. This method allows for more immediate recording.

➢ For the following session, ask the child to record in his *Coping cat workbook* one anxious experience and one non-anxious experience, describing what happened, how the child knew he was anxious, how he felt, and what he thought.

➢ Ask the child to write down what happened as precisely as possible and to add any additional information he wishes. Ask the child to enter information into his *workbook* as soon as possible after the experience, when it is fresh.

➢ If appropriate, the therapist models recording a STIC situation for the child. The therapist imagines herself in an anxiety-provoking situation and writing a description of the imaged experience. The therapist asks the child to imagine himself in a situation as the therapist describes it and records the event in the way he will be recording his actual experiences.

➢ Take a few minutes to engage in a fun activity at the end of the session.

Tips from the Trenches

Session 2

➢ All **concepts can be introduced by first referring to other people** rather than focusing on the child's own feelings or experiences. For example, the therapist can discuss how the child knows what friends or family members are feeling based on their facial expressions and body postures. Begin with people who are familiar to the child without having to focus immediately on the child's own specific concerns.

➢ Sometimes the therapist may notice distress in the child even when the therapist is only role-playing her own experiences with anxiety. These children tend to have difficulty differentiating their own emotional experience from the experiences of others around them. In such cases, **proceed slowly toward independent role play using the "tag-along" procedure.**

➢ The therapist can **talk about how animals show their fear**, for example, how a cat's hair stands on end or how a dog puts his tail between his legs. Mentioning that even animals sometimes get nervous or scared helps to normalize anxiety.

➢ **Act out different emotions and their somatic responses** (e.g., stomachache) as a fun way for the child to learn the session material. Acting silly during role-plays can ease the child's own self-conscious feelings and foster creativity, while setting a nice precedent for future sessions.

➢ When beginning to build the fear hierarchy, **it is helpful for the therapist to have an idea in advance of the situations the child may want to put on the hierarchy** (usually gathered at an initial or intake assessment). If the child is having difficulty thinking of situations to put on the hierarchy, the therapist can mention some ideas specific to the child by suggesting that "other kids I work with have been anxious about ____, is that something you would like to work on too?"

➢ **Stories about an imaginary group of kids in a stressful situation may be particularly helpful** with younger or lower functioning children who may have difficulty describing/generating situations in which they feel anxious.

Identifying Somatic Responses to Anxiety
Session 3

Purpose

Review distinguishing anxious/worried feelings from other types of feelings. Have the child learn more about somatic responses to anxiety and to identify his own specific somatic responses to anxiety.

Goals

1. Review STIC task from Session 2
2. Discuss specific somatic reactions to anxiety
3. Practice identifying somatic responses
4. Introduce the "F" step
5. Prepare the child for the upcoming parent session
6. Assign STIC task

Tasks

1. **Review STIC task from Session 2**

   ➢ Encourage the child to share the experiences he recorded. In particular, focus the discussion on the somatic feelings that he experienced during these episodes. Reward with stickers or points for STIC completion. If the STIC was not completed, do it with the child at the start of the session.

2. **Discuss specific somatic reactions to anxiety**

   ➢ Introduce the variety of somatic feelings that are associated with anxiety including butterflies in the stomach, heart beating fast, flushing of the face, trembling, etc., by telling a story about people caught in an anxiety-provoking situation and how each one feels during the experience.

   ➢ Ask the child to identify the kinds of somatic responses he has heard about, or that he experienced when in an anxiety-provoking situation. If the child is not able to be specific, suggest that he imagine himself in a safe and neutral situation, imagining how his body feels. The therapist then describes a situation, which is anxiety-provoking for the child, and again asks him to describe how his body feels. Ask the child to describe what his body felt in the anxiety-provoking situation which he did not feel in the safe, neutral situation. This effort is intended to make the somatic signs of anxiety more apparent and clear. Describing the experiences of other people can also help.

3. **Practice identifying somatic responses**   FLEX

   ➢ Using coping modeling and role play procedures
   Using imaginal procedures, the therapist sets up a low-anxiety situation and models recognition of her own physical responses (i.e., "There's that feeling in my stomach again!"). The therapist uses the "Feelings Thermometer" to record her own level of anxiety. Keep in mind that a "coping model" doesn't demonstrate initial success, but intentionally demonstrates a problem like that experienced by the child, strategies to overcome the problem, and then some success.

The therapist again sets up a low anxiety-provoking situation, but this time the child is asked to role play the situation with the therapist in a tag-along procedure. As the therapist describes her feelings she asks the child if he is feeling the same thing or if he is feeling something different. Validate the child's own feelings.

Finally the child is asked to role play a situation in which he feels only low levels of anxiety, without the therapist modeling (with prompts, as needed). The therapist encourages the child to identify his somatic responses verbally during the role play and to review them following the role play. The therapist encourages the child's participation in setting up the role-play situation and can skip some of the tag-along procedures for children who catch on quickly. At the same time, for children who find the role play difficult, the therapist steps in and goes back to coping modeling or tag-along procedures. Also, some avoidant children may be more comfortable using puppets when providing the dialogue. Especially at the beginning, the emphasis is on increasing the child's participation.

FLEX

➢ In situations that are more stressful
Coping modeling and role-play procedures are followed with discussion of situations that seem to provoke slightly higher levels of anxiety for the child, again focusing on the child's somatic responses. The therapist can point out in a sensitive way any signs of anxiety, such as flushing or fidgeting, that the child might not have recognized or reported. The child is asked to compare the differences in feelings between the low levels of anxiety and the higher levels.

If at any time during these procedures, it is difficult for the child to cope with his anxiety, the therapist instructs the child to "freeze frame"—to stop the situation—and take a deep breath. The therapist can also lead the child through several relaxation exercises (relaxation training is more formally introduced in Session 5).

> As cues to increasing anxiety

Discuss with the child the fact that his somatic responses can be a helpful signal to him that he is becoming anxious and that knowledge of the presence of his anxiety can help him know when to use the coping skills he will learn in later sessions.

4.   Introduce the "F" step

> The therapist introduces the child to the idea of a 4-step coping plan, called the FEAR plan. The first step, the "F" step is:

Feeling Frightened?

E

A

R

As part of the "F" step, the child distinguishes anxious feelings, monitors his somatic responses associated with the anxiety, and asks himself, "Am I feeling frightened?," "How does my body feel?"

5.   Prepare the child for the upcoming parent session

> The child is reminded that the next meeting will be held with his parents. The therapist reassures the child that she will not share during the parent session personal information he has disclosed. For example the therapist asks the child "Is there anything you don't want me to talk about"? The therapist informs the child that she is interested in what his parents think about the treatment and how they can be of help.

6.   Assign STIC task

> The child's STIC task is to pay attention to his body's reaction to anxiety two times during the week and to record in his *Coping cat workbook* what his body felt. The therapist asks the child to rate his anxiety in each situation based on the feelings in his body using the feelings thermometer. The therapist reminds the child to bring his STIC task to the next child session.

> At the end of the session, take a few minutes to play a game or engage in a fun activity.

Tips from the Trenches

Session 3

➤ The STIC task review provides the therapist an opportunity to **review past concepts** and to introduce the concepts to be presented in the current session.

➤ **The therapist can disclose anxious experiences of her own** during STIC tasks or at other times when asking the child to self-disclose. Recent or past experiences can help to normalize anxiety.

➤ **The therapist and child can engage in a "body drawing" activity.** On a large piece of butcher paper, the therapist and child draw an outline of a body or trace the child's body. The body is then "filled in" by drawing the various physical symptoms of anxiety that people experience (e.g., pounding heart, sweaty palms, lump in throat, etc.) The child and therapist take turns circling or labeling the physical symptoms that are specific to each of person.

➤ **The therapist and child can play a guessing game** to make learning about somatic responses more fun. The therapist and child can take turns guessing what emotion the other is feeling when their body reacts a certain way (acted out).

➤ **The therapist can use the "fire alarm" analogy to help explain the experience of somatic responses**. Physical symptoms warn us when there is danger. Sometimes, though, the alarm will go off when there is no emergency (false alarms) because the alarm system has malfunctioned, or is turned up too much. In these cases, the therapist will help the child to learn to "send back the fire trucks" because there is no danger. Keep it fun.

➤ **The anxiety rating scale can be a fire alarm indicator.** When it reaches a certain level, the alarm sounds: when you reach a certain level, that's when you know that it is time to do something or ask for help. This analogy gives the child a rationale for why we are paying attention to feelings.

First Meeting with Parents
Session 4

Purpose

Encourage parental cooperation in the treatment program. Answer parents' questions.

Goals

1. Provide additional information about treatment
2. Provide parents an opportunity to discuss their concerns
3. Learn more about the situations in which the child becomes anxious
4. Offer specific ways the parents can be involved in the program

Tasks

1. **<u>Provide additional information about treatment</u>**

➤ The therapist outlines the treatment program and explains (generally) where the child is in treatment and what will happen next. Parents' questions are invited and answered. The therapist reminds the parents that the first segment of the treatment is learning skills and that reduction in anxiety is not anticipated until the child begins to learn to apply coping skills during the second half of the treatment.

2. **<u>Provide parents an opportunity to discuss their concerns</u>**

➤ Invite parents to discuss their concerns about the child or about other factors that could affect the child's difficulties and ability to benefit from the treatment. With open-ended questions, the therapist invites the parents to provide any additional history or current information which they feel will be helpful to the therapist in understanding the child.

3. **<u>Learn more about the situations in which the child becomes anxious</u>**

➤ Using what has been learned in sessions to date, the therapist talks generally about her impressions of situations that are troublesome for the child and of the child's typical somatic and cognitive responses to anxiety. She invites the parents to share their impressions.

4. **<u>Offer specific ways the parents can be involved in the program</u>**

➤ The therapist invites the parents to sit in for a portion of Session 5 so that they can hear about and possibly assist in practicing relaxation skills. Parents are also given the option to call the therapist if they think of additional information, or if they have further questions. Depending on the age of the child and the quality of parental support, the therapist may ask for the parents' help in specific areas during the coming weeks.

Tips from the Trenches
Session 4

> When explaining the treatment program to the parents, **show the parents a blank *Coping cat workbook*** so the parents have a better understanding of the structure of the sessions.

> **Set expectations for therapy:** the goal is not the total elimination of anxiety, but the teaching of skills to know how and when to manage anxious arousal.

> **Set expectations about the child's self-disclosure:** parents do not need to report to the therapist every week about things that happened, or be concerned that the child doesn't report them himself. It takes time for the child to feel comfortable. Reminder: inform parents not to grill the child after each session to try to determine what was discussed.

> **Address any concerns the parents may feel** uncomfortable about sharing in front of the child.

> **Gather information about the parents understanding of anxiety.** This information helps to assess the extent to which the parents need to be educated about the nature and developmental course of child anxiety.

> After talking with the parents, it may be necessary to **teach the parents how to manage their child's anxiety and, if necessary, their own anxiety about the child**. The therapist normalizes the tendency for parents to want to protect or reassure their child or allow their child to avoid distressful situations. However, parents are informed about the "dangers of avoidance" by explaining that, over the long term, avoidance actually maintains anxiety. Explain that reinforcing "brave" behavior (through praise, rewards) is preferred. Also explain how parents are models of both "desirable" and "undesirable" behavior.

> **A therapist may want to explain "transfer of control:"** effective change involves a gradual transfer of the knowledge, skills, and methods from therapist to child and parent.

> It is important that the therapist **point out the strengths of the child** (instead of only talking about the child's anxiety) that may facilitate learning during treatment sessions (e.g., creativity).

Relaxation Training
Session 5

Purpose

Review recognizing the somatic cues that indicate that the child is tense and anxious. Introduce relaxation training and its use in controlling tension associated with anxiety.

Goals

1. Acknowledge the parent session
2. Review STIC task from Session 3
3. Introduce the idea that many somatic feelings associated with anxiety involve muscle tension
4. Introduce the idea of relaxation and practice relaxation techniques
5. Develop the child's awareness of how and when relaxation might be useful
6. Practice relaxation via coping modeling and role-play
7. Practice relaxation with the child's parents
8. Assign STIC task

Tasks

1. ## Acknowledge the parent session

   ➤ Mention to (remind) the child that you met with his parent(s) as planned. Reassure him that you could tell that his parents really care about him and that they are proud of his efforts. Encourage any questions the child may have about your meeting with his parents. Explain to the child that his parents, assuming it is OK with him, will be invited in for the last part of today's session so they can see how he is learning the new skill of relaxation and so they can help set up an opportunity for him to practice at home.

2. ## Review STIC task from Session 3

   ➤ Initiate a discussion with the child about the anxious experiences he described in his *Coping cat workbook*. Discuss these anxious experiences thoroughly, but particularly focus on the somatic responses that were experienced. If the child has not clearly described or has difficulty recalling somatic feelings associated with the two experiences, use an imaginal role play to help the child identify the physical expressions of his worried and anxious feelings. Reward the child with two points, if appropriate, and allow him to exchange his accumulated points for a prize at the end of the session. If the STIC was not completed, do it with the child at the start of the session.

3. ## Introduce the idea that many somatic feelings associated with anxiety involve muscle tension

   ➤ Suggest that when a person becomes anxious, some parts of his body are tense or tight and that the somatic responses are linked to that tension.

4. ## Introduce the idea of relaxation and practice relaxation techniques

   ➤ Imagine feeling relaxed
   Ask the child to think of a time or situation in which he was really calm and happy. Ask him to imagine himself in that scene and to focus on how his body feels.

➢ Imagine feeling tense

Now, describe an anxiety provoking situation and ask the child to imagine himself in that scene. The child is instructed to pay attention to his somatic responses so that he will know which parts of his body become tense.

➢ Compare feeling tense to feeling relaxed

Discuss with the child the difference between how his body feels when it is tense and when it is relaxed. Reinforce this idea by asking the child to make a tight fist by clenching his hand while the therapist counts to five and to focus on how it feels (for younger children, you can pretend to "squeeze a lemon"). Then tell the child to relax his fist to the count of five and to focus on the warm, relaxed feeling in his hand. Note to the child that if he can learn to relax the tense parts of his body, he will be taking the first step in coping with his anxiety.

➢ Deep breathing

Dim the lights in the room and have the child find a comfortable position (e.g., lying on a couch, lounging in a bean bag). Tell the child that you will be doing an exercise to help him learn to relax and ask the child to close his eyes. The first relaxation skill to be introduced is deep breathing. The child is told to take a deep breath and try to make his stomach expand (like blowing up a balloon), then to let it out slowly, focusing on how his body feels as the air comes out. The procedure is repeated 3 to 5 times. Ask the child to focus on how his body feels after taking a few deep breaths, noticing the relaxed feelings and suggesting that this is one quick way to help feel relaxed. Suggest that this idea ("taking a deep breath.") may be quite useful as a first coping strategy in an anxiety-provoking situation.

➢ Progressive muscle relaxation

Again ask the child to tighten his fist to the count of 5 and then relax it to the count of 5, focusing on the relaxed warm feeling in his hand, following it into his arm and continuing to follow it as it works its way through his body. Continue the relaxation exercise, focusing on the two or three muscle groups which the child has identified (or the therapist has noticed) as the areas in which the child experiences tension.

It is wise to limit the number of new muscle groups that are to be introduced to two or three. The exercise lasts approximately 15 minutes, as it is unlikely that the child will be able to focus on the activity any longer.

The therapist may choose to use the Feelings Thermometer (SUDS rating) to track the progress of the child's relaxation.

FLEX

➢ Relaxation materials/aids

To help children begin to identify the difference between how their body feels and looks when it is tense versus when it is relaxed, the exercises on pp. 17-19 of the *Coping cat workbook* are used.

When practicing relaxation skills, a script which puts the exercises in a story-like scenario (e.g., Koeppen, 1974) encourages participation and practice for younger children. For the older child, see Ollendick and Cerny's (1981) relaxation script. Also, the *I Can Relax!* CD *for Children* (The Child Anxiety Network, 2001) is a useful tool and fun way to introduce relaxation procedures.

In addition, the therapist, using her own voice, records the relaxation procedures on a CD or audiotape and provides the child with a special CD/tape to take home so that he can practice his relaxation skills on his own. On the CD/tape, the therapist "walks" the child through the relaxation procedures such as deep breathing and progressive muscle relaxation.

5. **Develop the child's awareness of how/when relaxation might be useful**

➢ Explain that relaxation training exercises are done to help the child realize what it feels like to be tense or relaxed and to help to relax more quickly. Explain that under real life anxious circumstances he usually won't have the opportunity to do a thorough relaxation exercise, but probably could take a few deep breaths and concentrate on relaxing those muscle groups that he has come to recognize he tends to tighten when anxious.

6. **Practice relaxation via coping modeling and role-play**

➤ The therapist describes an anxiety-provoking scenario and models recognition of anxious feelings and accompanying tension by talking about her somatic responses. Be a coping model! Demonstrate coping by modeling the unwanted stress (and thoughts) and then using the deep breaths and relaxing. Describe carefully what is being done. The child tags along with the therapist during a similar sequence, or the child can role-play a similar sequence while the therapist only provides prompts as needed.

7. **Practice relaxation with the child's parents**

➤ When the child and therapist have gone through the exercises, the therapist
FLEX reminds the child that he can "show-off" these new skills to his parents. The parents are invited into the session for the final 10-15 minutes and the child or therapist briefly explains the rationale for relaxation training. The therapist invites the parents to participate if they wish and with the child repeats the exercise script (the child demonstrates relaxation).

8. **Assign STIC task**

➤ The therapist explains the need for daily relaxation practice, describing the ability to relax as a skill to be learned, not something that can be done automatically. The child is asked to do the breathing and muscle tightening and relaxing exercises introduced during the session. When appropriate, parents are asked to assist in helping the child find a time and place to practice. If there are siblings, the child could choose to have them join in the practice or he could choose a private place and/or headphones to practice with his CD/tape. The goals are to (a) practice at least once a day for several days and (b) write about 2 anxiety-provoking situations including any thoughts and somatic cues he identifies.

➤ At the end of the session, take a few minutes to play a game or engage in a fun activity.

Tips from the Trenches

Session 5

➤ **The therapist can gently point out to the child the muscle tightness that she may have noticed in him**, even if the child was not aware of it.

➤ Some kids are nervous or feel uncomfortable when the therapist is beginning the relaxation procedure. Assure the child that it might seem strange at first, but **relaxation will get easier with practice.** In some cases, the therapist might want to face away from the child so that the child feels more comfortable engaging in the relaxation exercises.

➤ To facilitate the process, **the therapist can do the exercises along with the child.** The therapist would record the practice CD/tape before the session and then play the CD/tape during the session so both can follow along.

➤ **Record the child's relaxation CD/tape prior to the session** to ensure that the recording is free from unwanted distractions/deviations that can occur during the session.

➤ The therapist can **experiment with different relaxation scripts and strategies** (e.g., meditation, guided imagery) and focus on the techniques the child prefers.

➤ Reminder: **the exercise is used to teach the child how relaxed muscles feel as compared to tense muscles.** The child is encouraged to practice so he is eventually able to make his muscles feel relaxed without using the exercise itself. Once he can achieve relaxation without tensing first, he is able to become relaxed inconspicuously in any environment. Practice, practice, practice!

➤ **Explaining the relaxation procedure to parents** of younger children will help the children remember the steps and remember to practice. Older children may prefer that the therapist not discuss this with his parents and feel more comfortable practicing alone, without parental involvement.

Identifying Anxious Self-Talk and Learning to Challenge Thoughts
Session 6

Purpose

Introduce the function of personal thoughts and their impact on response in anxiety-provoking situations. Help the child begin to recognize his self-talk (expectations, automatic questions, and attributions) in anxious situations. Help the child begin to develop and use coping self-talk. Review relaxation training.

Goals

1. Review STIC task from Session 5
2. Introduce the concept of thoughts (self-talk)
3. Discuss self-talk in anxiety-provoking situations (anxious self-talk)
4. Differentiate anxious self-talk from coping self-talk
5. Introduce the "E" step
6. Practicing coping self-talk
7. Assign STIC task

Tasks

1. **Review STIC task from Session 5**

   ➤ Discuss the child's experiences when practicing relaxing, noting the parts that went well and those that did not. Initiate a discussion with the child about his experiences recording the anxiety-provoking situations during the intervening days. Focus on anxious and non-anxious somatic feelings (to reinforce the skills from Sessions 3 and 5). Listen for any suggestion from the child of thoughts or expectations associated with these experiences and, in age-appropriate terms, call them to his attention. Reward the child with 2 points as appropriate. If the STIC was not completed, do it with the child at the start of the session. **FLEX**

   ➤ Take 10 minutes to do relaxation, reviewing old muscle groups and adding new ones (recording them on the CD/tape). Discuss the child's experiences using relaxation as his first response when becoming anxious, and expand on the idea of a quick relaxation exercise such as a few deep breaths and relaxing the muscles he tends to tighten.

2. **Introduce the concept of thoughts (self-talk)**

   Suggest to the child that now he knows when he becomes anxious, and that there are some thoughts that probably occur along with the feelings.

   FLEX

   ➤ Thought-bubble activity

   Show cartoons with empty bubbles (see pp. 22-24 in the *Coping cat workbook*). Together with the therapist, the child fills in the possible thoughts for different cartoons. The cartoons portray fairly simple scenes in which the character's thoughts are likely to be fairly obvious and include a number of different types of feelings.

   ➤ Self-talk in low-stress (concrete) situations

   The therapist describes some fairly concrete and non-stressful, or slightly stressful, situations (e.g., "your pencil falls on the floor" or "your mother is serving broccoli for dinner and you hate broccoli"). The child is asked to give

29

some samples of thoughts that would accompany these events (i.e., "What would be in your bubble?"). The child thinks of a situation and describes what thoughts might occur to someone else who just experienced that situation.

> Self-talk in low-stress, ambiguous situations
Present a non-stressful but fairly ambiguous situation (i.e., thoughts will vary from coping thoughts to negative thoughts), and the therapist works to suggest and illustrate that depending on which thought a person had, his behavior could vary. Presented with an ambiguous situation (e.g., roller blading), the child is asked to develop two different thoughts and describe the likely variation in behavior because of those different thoughts (e.g., pp. 24-26 in the *Coping cat workbook*).

3. **Discuss self-talk in anxiety-provoking situations (anxious self-talk)**

> Using cartoons (or magazine pictures) to present characters in low-anxiety-provoking situations (select a cartoon/picture of specific interest to the child), the therapist suggests possible thoughts that the character might have and then asks the child to make similar suggestions for other cartoons/pictures. The therapist makes a connection between the thought "something bad is going to happen" and anxious feelings.

FLEX

4. **Differentiate anxious self-talk from coping self-talk** FLEX

> Again, present cartoons (or magazine pictures) depicting a character in a low-anxiety-provoking situation, but this time ask the child to help think of thoughts that (a) would lead the character to experience more distress (i.e., anxious self-talk) and (b) would help the character to reduce distress (i.e., coping self-talk). Using this example, the therapist introduces the idea of coping self-talk, or thoughts that help people reduce distress in anxious situations. The therapist and child discuss how the character might change his behavior depending on the way he thought about what had happened: The child and therapist change the "talk" in the thought bubble and have the end result of the cartoon sequence/picture change accordingly.

5. Introduce the "E" step

> Introduces the child to the second step to the "E" step:

Feeling Frightened?

Expecting bad things to happen?

A

R

Explain that as part of the "E" step, the child monitors his thoughts associated with anxiety and asks himself, "What is my self-talk?" "What am I expecting to happen?" Illustrate how if someone is thinking negative thoughts, the person can then attempt to reduce his distress through changing the self-talk to coping self-talk. Inform the child that the other 2 steps in the FEAR plan will be learned in later sessions.

6. Practicing coping self-talk

> Practice using the first 2-steps in the FEAR plan

The therapist models, and the child tags along, practicing the "E" step and monitoring thoughts in increasing anxiety-provoking situations, going through the following questions:

Feeling frightened?

+ Ask myself:
  Am I feeling anxious? What's happening in my body?

Expecting bad things to happen?

+ Ask myself:
  What is my self-talk? What am I expecting to happen?
+ Gather evidence for the thought (be a detective!):
  Do I know for sure this is going to happen? What else might happen? What has happened before? Has this happened to anyone I know? How many times has it happened before?
+ Having collected all the evidence:
  How likely is it to happen? What is a coping thought I can have in this situation? What is the worst thing that could happen? What would be so bad about that?

> Discuss thinking traps

Encourage the child to be a detective and look for thinking traps that can trick people into feeling anxious before they have had a chance to collect evidence.

- **Walking with blinders**
  Only seeing the negative and overlooking the good in a situation
  [Race horses wear "blinders" to see straight and not be distracted in a race]

- **The repetitor**
  If it happened once it is always going to happen that way

- **The catastrophiser (or the pessimist)**
  Always thinking the 'worst ever' is going to happen

- **The avoider**
  Staying away from situations you think are scary without trying first

- **The mind reader (or fortune-teller, using the "crystal ball")**
  Jumping to conclusions about a person/thing/situation without the facts

- **The shoulds (having "the shoulds" is like having "a cold")**
  I SHOULD always be perfect. I SHOULDN'T make mistakes.

- **The perfectionist**
  Setting expectations that are too high: Perfection is not a human option.

> Make a "coping card" FLEX

Encourage the child to make a card of potential coping thoughts and/or good prompt or "detective" questions to take with him into anxiety-provoking situations. For younger children, a card with an image to represent their coping thought may also be useful.

7. Assign STIC task

> During the next week, the child is asked to record in the *Coping cat workbook* two situations in which he felt anxious and pay special attention to his thoughts. Remind the child to practice listening to his relaxation CD/tape and to record his experiences.

> At the end of the session, take a few minutes to play a game or engage in a fun activity.

Tips from the Trenches

Session 6

➢ To help the child identify his anxious self-talk, the **therapist can ask the child to draw a picture of himself in an anxious situation and then draw thought bubbles over the pictures** that can be filled in. This activity may be especially useful for artistic/creative children or children who tend to have difficulty verbalizing their thoughts and/or emotions.

➢ For older children, it may be useful to illustrate the idea of self-talk by **providing examples of television shows in which the main character is the narrator** (e.g., Lizzie Maguire, the Wonder Years, Scrubs, etc.)

➢ The **therapist checks with the child about whether he believes his coping thoughts**, because the child may be able to think of alternatives but not believe they are valid. A child may need to be encouraged to generate thoughts that are non-distressing and relevant to the particular situation, and to be assisted in seeing their true merits

➢ Children can also **identify imaginary or real people whom they admire as "good at coping"** and use them as models. At times, if the client cannot generate coping thoughts, or is unwilling to consider other possibilities, he can think about how the hero or "good coper" might think differently.

➢ Caution: **Be careful not to fall in the trap of trying to convince the child that a scary event is not likely to happen**. A good strategy is for the therapist and child to reverse roles—have the child "act" the part of the coach or detective and try to convince the therapist that a situation is unlikely to happen. It is also helpful to discuss with the child what might be done if his worst possible fear ever does come true.

➢ The therapist and child can **make a shorter or longer list of thinking traps** (renaming them to fit), highlighting the ones typically used by someone the child knows, or by the child himself. When apt, the child can take the list home and post it on the refrigerator so that he is reminded of the potential "traps."

Reviewing Anxious and Coping Self-Talk and Developing Problem Solving Skills
Session 7

Purpose

Review the concept of anxious self-talk and reinforce changing anxious self-talk into coping self-talk. Introduce the concept of problem solving and develop and use problem solving strategies to better manage anxiety. Review relaxation training.

Goals

1. Review STIC task from Session 6
2. Review and discuss the first 2 steps in the FEAR plan
3. Introduce the "A" step
4. Discuss the concept of problem solving
5. Practice problem solving in anxious situations
6. Assign STIC task

Tasks

1. **<u>Review STIC task from Session 6</u>**

   ➢ Discuss with the child the anxious experiences he described in his *Coping cat workbook*. Focus the discussion on how the child knew he was anxious and what his anxious self-talk was, using a modified version of the "triple-column" procedure. Three columns headed "Situation," "Feelings," and "Thoughts" are written, leaving space for adding a fourth column. During the discussion, the therapist writes the information in the appropriate column, thereby helping the child organize his thoughts about his experiences. A fourth column entitled "Actions" is added, and possible alternative actions which might be related to different entries in the "Thoughts" column are entered. Reward the child for effort and cooperation with two points or stickers, as appropriate. If the STIC was not completed, do it with the child at the start of the session.

   ➢ Discuss the child's experiences during the week practicing relaxation, noting both the times that went well and those in which he experienced difficulty.

   FLEX → Take a few minutes to do a relaxation training exercise. Discuss the child's experiences using relaxation as a first response when becoming anxious, and expand on the idea of a quick relaxation exercise such as a few deep breaths and relaxing the muscles he tends to tighten.

2. **<u>Review and discuss the first 2 steps in the FEAR plan</u>**

   ➢ The therapist summarizes the two previously introduced steps by reminding the child that now he realizes that his body responds with certain feelings when he is becoming anxious, and that there is anxious self-talk. Use an experience that was recorded in the four-column procedure as an example and encourage the child to think of other examples.

   ➢ Suggest to the child that he can begin to take steps to change his responses in an anxious situation. Recognizing the responses his body has to anxiety and identifying anxious self-talk are the first two steps in learning to proceed in a situation in spite of feeling anxious.

➤ The therapist suggests to the child that when he is in an anxious, worrisome situation, it will be easier to manage his anxiety if he knows what steps to follow. Encourage the child to generate the first two steps based on his work thus far. These steps are explained below in a general way, but are phrased in the child's own language. Write the first two steps on a black/whiteboard for the child to refer to throughout the session.

Feeling frightened?

➤ Ask myself:
Am I feeling anxious? What's happening in my body?

Expecting bad things to happen?

➤ Ask myself:
What is my self-talk? What am I expecting to happen?
➤ Gather evidence for the thought (be a detective!):
Do I know for sure this is going to happen? What else might happen? What has happened before? Has this happened to anyone I know? How many times has it happened before?
➤ Having collected all the evidence:
How likely is it to happen? What is a coping thought I can have in this situation? What is the worst thing that could happen? What would be so bad about that?

3. **Introduce the "A" Step**

➤ The therapist introduces the child to the third step to coping with anxiety in the FEAR plan, the "A" step:

Feeling Frightened?

Expecting bad things to happen?

Attitudes and actions that can help

R

The therapist explains to the child that that in addition to recognizing his anxious feelings and self-talk, he may find it helpful to take some action that will help change the situation so he can proceed despite his anxiety. The final step in the coping plan will be learned in Session 8.

36

4. **Discuss the concept of problem solving**

  ➢ Describe the problem-solving steps

The therapist explains that problem solving helps to develop a plan for coping with the anxiety (This plan will be specific to the type of situation and the child's particular preference for strategies that are helpful to him). Discuss the problem solving process by describing for the child how to develop an idea for changing something, using the following steps:

Step 1

   ✦ Define the problem:
      What is the anxious situation?

Step 2

   ✦ Explore potential alternative solutions (be careful not to evaluate yet!):
      What might someone do to make this situation less fearful?

Step 3

   ✦ Evaluate the potential alternative solutions:
      Which solutions are feasible alternatives?
      Do any alternative solutions NOT make sense or are any NOT feasible?

Step 4

   ✦ Select the preferred alternative:
      What might be one of the best things to do?
      What is the preferred solution?

This presentation will have to be modified to accommodate the child's developmental level, particularly in terms of the language and cognitive ability. Some children will be able to understand and comprehend the ideas as presented, but the language level will have to be lowered. For young children, the procedure may simply have to be taught by example and practice.

  ➢ Apply problem solving to nonstressful situations

To demonstrate how to use this method of developing an idea, begin with a simple, non-stressful problem which is concrete and real for the child (e.g., "You've lost your shoes somewhere is your house. How might you go about trying to find them?"). The therapist models the process of exploring the alternatives and selecting the preferred alternative first.

The therapist then sets up another very concrete situation and will again model this process, but this time the child is encouraged to participate in the problem-solving process by contributing suggestions and evaluating them for the best one. Throughout this exercise, the therapist takes care to emphasize that this skill takes much practice and that the child should not expect to be good at it right away.

5. **Practice problem solving in anxious situations**

> Practice under conditions of minimal anxiety
Practice the same process in low anxiety-provoking situations. Again, the therapist models problem solving first and then invites the child to tag-along. As always, the child is encouraged to contribute his own scenarios to be acted out, but the therapist is also prepared with relevant situations if the child does not contribute ideas.

> Practice under conditions involving greater anxiety
The problem solving activity is applied to higher anxiety-provoking situations, again using therapist modeling and child tag-along procedures as needed until the child can think through a situation with too many therapist prompts.

6. **Assign STIC task**

> During the next week, the child is asked to record in the *Coping cat workbook* two situations in which he felt anxious and to pay special attention to his actions in these situations. Also, the child is reminded to continue to listen to his relaxation CD/tape (although this week the child is not asked to record his experiences).

> At the end of the session, take a few minutes to play a game or engage in a fun activity.

Tips from the Trenches

Session 7

➤ Keep in mind that **brainstorming is done without evaluative comment.** The merits of the various options are not examined until after the list is done—we don't want to inhibit the child nor discredit a good idea before giving it a chance.

➤ It's a **good idea for the therapist to have some suggestions in mind when considering alternative solutions**. Here are a few: try to change the situation (instrumental coping); yell or cry (emotional intervention); distraction (think about something else); think differently (coping thoughts); seek emotional support (family, friends); do nothing.

➤ To **integrate information from previous sessions**, the therapist can choose a few of the thought bubble pictures from Session 6 that demonstrate potentially anxiety-provoking situations (e.g., a girl dropping her lunch tray) and the child and therapist can attempt to recall the "thoughts" from last session, challenge those thoughts, generate coping thoughts, and problem solve about how to make the situation less-anxiety-provoking for the child in the picture. Remember that it is easier for the child to practice when talking about someone else (child in the cartoon).

Introducing Self-Evaluation and Self-Reward and Reviewing Skills Already Learned
Session 8

Purpose

Introduce the concept of evaluating or rating performance and rewarding yourself based on effort and performance. Review all previously introduced skills by formalizing the 4-step FEAR plan for the child to use when feeling anxious and practicing its use in non-stressful situations.

Goals

1. Review STIC task from Session 7
2. Introduce the "R" step
3. Discuss the concept of self-rating and reward
4. Practice making self-ratings and rewarding oneself for effort
5. Review the FEAR plan
6. Apply the FEAR plan
7. Review the fear hierarchy and discuss exposure tasks
8. Acknowledge upcoming parent session
9. Assign STIC task

Tasks

1. **Review STIC task from Session 7**

   ➤ Initiate a discussion about the child's experience during the intervening days. Have the child describe his experience developing a plan of action when faced with an anxious situation--be sure to encourage and support even partial successes. Remind the child that mastering these skills requires lots of practice. Reward him for his effort and cooperation with points, as appropriate. If the STIC was not completed, do it with the child at the start of the session.

   ➤ Discuss the child's experiences during the week practicing relaxation, noting both the times that went well and those in which he experienced difficulty. Discuss the child's experiences using relaxation as his first response when becoming anxious, and expand on the idea of a quick relaxation exercise such as a few deep breaths and relaxing the muscles he tends to tighten.

   FLEX

2. **Introduce the "R" step**

   ➤ The therapist introduces the child to the final step to coping with anxiety in the FEAR plan, the "R" step:

   > **F**eeling Frightened?
   > **E**xpecting bad things to happen?
   > **A**ttitudes and actions that can help
   > **R**esults and rewards

   Summarize for the child the first three steps of recognizing his anxious feelings, recognizing his anxious self-talk and applying coping self-talk, and taking some action that will help change the situation. Introduce the idea of rating his performance and rewarding himself for efforts to cope and to stay in a situation despite his anxiety.

3. **Discuss the concept of self-rating and reward**

   ➤ Describe self-rating and rewards

   The therapist begins the discussion by describing a reward as something that is given when you're pleased with the work that was done. Give examples of reward using a story about teaching a dog a trick: If the dog learns the trick, he gets a reward such as a dog biscuit, a pat on the head, or something else he enjoys. But the whole trick isn't learned all at once—it takes gradual steps that get closer and closer to the complete trick. If a puppy has trouble learning a trick, his trainer tries again and again until he gets it right. Emphasize the point that in the beginning the master might reward the puppy for doing part of the trick and that the puppy is rewarded each time he does something right.

Extend the concept to people by talking about "bosses" at work and evaluation and rewards (or another similar example that the child suggests) and discuss how a person feels after a reward or after being punished.

Introduce the idea of self-rating by describing how a child can decide whether or not he is satisfied with his own work. Suggest that people can rate themselves and reward or punish themselves for their own behavior. Provide concrete examples, drawn from your knowledge of the child's own experiences. For instance, for a Little Leaguer, "Imagine that you hit a single that scored a run and helped your team win the game. Were you successful at what you tried to do? How would you feel? What would you do afterwards? What would you be thinking about?" Be sure to point out that it would not be reasonable to expect to get a hit every time you are at bat (e.g., best hitters bat 1 for 3; average .330), and not always getting a hit is not justification to punish yourself. All that is asked is that one tries his best. Do the same for a scenario in which the child is not successful, so has no reward.

➤ Make a list of possible rewards for the child FLEX
Discuss with the child appropriate reward sizes (not too big), point out that rewards work best when they are immediate, and encourage a mix of material (e.g., trading cards) and nonmaterial (reading a book) rewards. Introduce the idea of social reward, such as going to a movie with friends or

playing a game with someone. Potential rewards are entered on p. 37 of the *Coping cat workbook* or into the "reward menu" on p. 73 of the *workbook.*

➢ Illustrate the use of self-rating and reward with examples (see p. 38 of the *Coping cat workbook)*. Present a scenario in which a child copes successfully with a fairly simple problem and rates himself positively (let the child steer the discussion whenever there is interest and involvement). Introduce the idea that how you feel afterwards indicates how you rated your performance—positive or negative. If you feel badly, chances are you were disappointed in your performance, but if you feel happy afterwards, you were probably happy with your efforts. Use the scenario to illustrate this idea by focusing on how the child feels afterwards. Also present a scenario in which a child has to face a more difficult situation where his actions can have little impact on solving the problem, but where he can nevertheless feel good or bad about his thoughts and responses to the situation. Discuss the difference to help the child see that it is possible to rate himself positively in spite of an unfavorable outcome that was beyond his control.

➢ Present the idea of a "Feelings Barometer"
Using the Feelings Barometer (p. 78 of the *workbook)*, the child measures his own rating of his/her effort/performance. The therapist models self-rating and uses the Feelings Barometer regarding a situation of her own. The therapist then presents a scenario and the child imagines himself in that scenario, and uses the Feelings Barometer to rate his effort/performance.

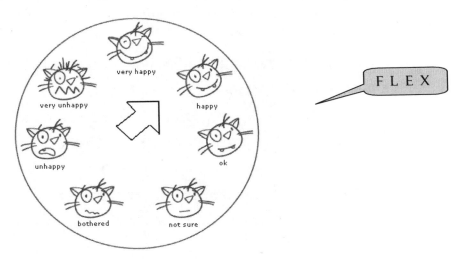

4. **<u>Practice making self-ratings and rewarding oneself for effort</u>** FLEX

➤ Therapist as a coping model

The therapist provides a coping model by describing at least one scenario in which she experienced some distress, did not automatically solve the problem, but nevertheless successfully coped with the anxiety, positively rated herself, and gave herself an appropriate reward. Examples of rewards considered might include telling herself she did a good job, writing about the accomplishment in her journal, sharing it with a friend, or spending time on a favorite hobby.

➤ Role-play

The therapist and child role play a scenario involving an anxious situation that is coped with successfully (not perfectly), using the "tag-along" procedure as necessary. Examples of possible self-rewards are included. Finally, the child role plays a similar scenario with less of the therapist's guidance. Remember that it's not enough to talk about these issues; provide the opportunity for real practice by orchestrating in role-play activities.

➤ Cartoon strips

The therapist presents the child with a cartoon strip in which the character attempts to cope with an anxiety-provoking situation and is successful. By the way, it is a good idea to have cartoon strips prepared ahead of time. The child is asked to fill in the thought bubbles.

The therapist can introduce a cartoon strip in which the character attempts to cope with an anxiety-provoking situation, but is only partially successful. The child is asked to fill in the thought bubbles. The therapist uses this opportunity to emphasize to the child that when he rates his own performance, he is likely to find both successes and things that could have been done better--people rarely do everything entirely correctly. Emphasize to the child that he can reward himself for effort and for progress—not just the times when he does something correctly. Focus on the idea that no one does everything perfectly and not doing something 100% correctly does not mean that you punish yourself (e.g., Michael Jordon shot 49%, lifetime shooting average).

The therapist describes at least one scenario in which the character does something well but would like to do other things better, demonstrating self-reward for partial success (perfection is not needed for reward). The child is encouraged to participate with the therapist in role playing a similar scenario.

The therapist then describes a scenario in which the character copes well with his anxious feelings, but the outcome is negative despite his best efforts, demonstrating self-reward for successful use of the 4-step plan even in the case of negative results.

5. Review the FEAR plan

➢ The therapist and child review the concepts in the 4-step FEAR plan and create a **"FEAR Plan ID"**—a pocket/wallet-sized index card such as the one on p. 79 of the *workbook*. The first letters of each FEAR step is emphasized in some colorful way. The child decorates the card creatively and personalizes the card with coping thoughts, possible rewards, etc. The therapist provides the crayons, markers, and stickers, laminates the card, and gives the child the card to carry with him.

> **FLEX**

➢ The FEAR acronym makes recall of the steps easier and facilitates successful coping. Children are encouraged to use the FEAR acronym during the sessions. If the child wants to be more creative, or has difficulty with the FEAR acronym, encourage him to generate his own acronym to remember the steps.

6. Apply the FEAR plan

➢ The therapist presents a somewhat stressful situation and then uses the FEAR acronym to help talk herself through the situation. The child and therapist participate together in a different scenario using the tag-along procedure (if necessary) and, finally, the child role plays his way through situations that are increasingly anxiety-provoking for him.

7. **Review the fear hierarchy and discuss exposure tasks**

   ➢ The therapist informs the child that the next session involves practicing the skills that have been learned. "We'll go places and do things." The following information may need to be discussed with the child:

   ✦ **The FEAR steps will be practiced in situations in which the child feels anxious or worried** (i.e., the situations identified on the situation cards/fear ladder in the *Coping cat workbook*). Practicing these steps in situations that provoke genuine anxiety allows the child to see that he can cope and to find out that what he thought was going to happen in the situation is unlikely to happen.

   ✦ **The practice will be carried out in a gradual way.** The child will start practicing in situations that make him only a little anxious (i.e. the Easy situation cards/bottom of fear ladder). Step by step we'll move up to approach some tougher situations (i.e. the Medium and Challenging situation cards/higher entries on the fear ladder). Once the child builds some confidence, we can try even tougher situations.

   ✦ **The aim of the treatment is not to remove the child's anxiety** all together but to reduce it to a normal level and to be able to manage it. It's like turning down a radio volume from a high volume of 10 to a normal volume of 2—the radio is still on, the volume is just lowered.

   ✦ **The child will experience some anxiety when practicing his skills,** but this is to be expected and is OK. The more he practices facing these situations the less anxious he will feel, and the more his mastery and confidence will build.

   ✦ **The fear steps need to be practiced repeatedly.** Facing situations that make the child feel anxious will be practiced over and over again. Practice will take place almost until the child feels bored with the situation rather than anxious. The practice is done both in and out of session.

   ✦ **Depending on the exposure task, the child may need to stay in the situation for a certain duration of time.** The aim of an exposure task is for the child to realize that he can cope with the situation and that what he thought was going to happen is not likely to happen. If he gets out of the situation too quickly, then he hasn't experienced that he can cope and the next time he enters the situation he will feel the same or even more anxiety.

➢ Using the situation cards or fear ladder in the *Coping cat workbook* (pp. 74-77), the therapist and child brainstorm a list of practice situations that are specific to the child's fears/worries. For example, a child with performance anxiety could be asked to read a poem to the therapist. In order to adequately design an exposure task, it is essential to ascertain the child's **feared outcome** in each situation. For example, designing an in-vivo for a child who is anxious at school because he is afraid he will have to answer a question in class will involve the child actually being asked a question and using the FEAR steps to cope with the experience. In this case, just practicing going to school will not allow the child to face the real situation. It is important to be as specific as possible when designing a hierarchy (see a list of exposure task suggestions in Kendall et al., 2005a).

➢ The therapist and child plan the first exposure task for Session 10, choosing something from the 'easy' cards or at the bottom of the fear ladder.

8. <u>Acknowledge upcoming parent session</u>

➢ Remind the child that the next meeting will be held with his parent(s). It is Ok to reassure the child that the therapist will not share personal information during the parental session. For example, the therapist can ask "Is there anything you don't want me to talk about when I meet with you parent(s)"? The therapist informs the child that she is interested in what his parents have to say and how they can be of help.

9. <u>Assign STIC task</u>

➢ Ask the child to record in his *workbook* two anxious situations that he experienced and to focus on self-rating and reward: whether he rated himself on partial success or just for total success, his feelings afterward, and what he used to reward himself.

➢ The child is also asked to explain the FEAR acronym to a parent, using the FEAR plan ID if needed. This experience helps the child understand the coping plan and also provides the parents with an understanding of the plan.

➢ At the end of the session, take a few minutes to play a game or engage in a fun activity.

Tips from the Trenches

Session 8

- For older children, using **analogies such as "a commission" for effort/sales at work**, or bigger and longer contracts for sports players based on performance may be useful to introduce the concept of reward based on effort.

- Anxious children set high standards and rarely reward themselves for their accomplishments and, instead, tend to rely on outside sources for this sense of achievement. **Encourage the child to feel proud of his accomplishments** and ask the child to describe for you a situation in which he felt proud of himself. Note to the child how someone (e.g., TV star) felt proud because he did something challenging.

- The therapist encourages the child to pick a favorite activity for both the child and therapist to do together following the session to **reward the child for his effort thus far in the treatment sessions.** Social rewards are terrific "together time." Be certain to allow time for the reward, and follow through on the plan.

- **Encourage the child to reward himself with positive self-statements** such as "I did a great job," or "I did it!" It may also be useful for the child to reward himself in situations where he is unable to provide himself with a material reward by imagining a pleasant event or scene. For example, when a child faces a stressful situation in school he can reward himself by imagining himself jumping up and down or doing a victory dance (e.g., a "touchdown" dance).

- With a younger client, it is helpful to have him **explain the 4-step coping plan to his parent(s)** in front of the therapist so that the therapist can assist if needed. For older children, it is suggested that the child talk to his parent(s) about the steps independently unless he wants the therapist there.

Second Meeting with Parents
Session 9

Purpose

Encourage continued parental cooperation in the treatment program. Answer parents' questions and address parental concerns.

Goals

1. Provide additional information about the second half of treatment (i.e., exposure tasks)
2. Provide parents an opportunity to discuss their concerns
3. Learn more about the situations in which the child becomes anxious
4. Offer specific ways the parents can be involved in the second half of treatment

Tasks

1. ## Provide additional information about the second half of treatment (i.e., exposure tasks)

   ➤ Provide a brief outline of the remainder of the treatment program and briefly explain the purpose and features of the second half of treatment. Explain that the child will be practicing the skills that he has learned. As presented to the child in Session 8, the following information is also presented to the parents. Parents' questions/concerns are invited and answered:

   - **The FEAR steps will be practiced in situations in which the child feels anxious or worried** (provide examples to parents of possible exposure tasks, both imaginal and in-vivo). Practicing these steps in situations that provoke genuine anxiety allows the child to see that he can cope and to find out that what he thought was going to happen in the situation is unlikely to happen.

   - **The practice will be carried out in a gradual way.** The child will start practicing, with the therapist, in situations that make him only a little anxious. Step by step he, along with his therapist, will approach some tougher situations. Once the child builds some confidence, he can try even tougher situations.

   - **The aim of the treatment is not to remove the child's anxiety** all together but to reduce it to a normal level and to be able to manage it. It's like turning down a radio volume from a high volume of 10 to a normal volume of 2—the radio is still on, the volume is just lowered.

   - **The child will experience some anxiety when practicing his skills,** but this is to be expected and is OK. The more he practices facing these situations the less anxious he will feel and the more his mastery and confidence will build.

   - **The fear steps need to be practiced repeatedly.** Facing situations that make the child feel anxious will be practiced over and over again. Practice will take place until the child feels bored with the situation rather than anxious. The practice is done both in and out of session.

   - **Depending on the exposure task, the child may need to stay in the situation for a certain duration of time.** The goal of practicing is for the child to realize that he can cope with the situation and that what he thought was going to happen is not likely to happen. If he gets out of the situation too quickly, then he hasn't experienced that he can cope and the next time he enters the situation he will feel the same or even more anxiety.

➤ After explaining the rationale behind the use of exposure tasks, the therapist acknowledges that this portion of the treatment may invoke some anxiety for the child before a reduction in anxiety is observed (i.e., anxiety may go up a bit before it comes way down). Spend time with the parents normalizing this process for them.

2. **Provide parents an opportunity to discuss their concerns**

➤ The therapist invites the parents to discuss their concerns about the child or about the child's participation in the second half of treatment, particularly the exposure tasks. With open-ended questions, invite the parents to provide any additional history or current information which they feel will be helpful in understanding the child and constructing useful exposure tasks.

3. **Learn more about the situations in which the child becomes anxious**

➤ Using what has been learned to date, talk generally about (a) impressions of situations that are troublesome for the child and (b) the child's typical somatic and cognitive responses to anxiety. Invite the parents to share their impressions and provide examples of situations in which they believe the child feels anxious and needs practice.

4. **Offer specific ways the parents can be involved in the second half of treatment**

➤ Invite the parents to assist in the execution of an exposure tasks, in session and at home, when appropriate/necessary. The parents are invited to call the therapist if they have additional helpful information or if they have further questions. Depending on the age of the child and the quality of parental support, the therapist may ask for the parents' help in other specific areas related to the child during the coming weeks.

Practicing in Low Anxiety-Provoking Situations Using Exposure Tasks
Session 10

Purpose

Practice the 4-step coping plan (i.e., the FEAR plan) under low anxiety-provoking conditions, both imaginal and in-vivo.

Goals

1. Review STIC task from Session 8
2. Review the idea of progressing from learning new skills to practicing new skills
3. Practice using imaginal exposure in low anxiety-provoking situations
4. Practice in-vivo exposure task in low anxiety-provoking situations
5. Briefly review relaxation exercises
6. Plan an exposure task(s) for Session 11
7. Assign STIC task

Tasks

1. **Review STIC task from Session 8**
   - Initiate a discussion about the intervening days with respect to the child's anxiety—how he's improving in terms of coping and managing it and how he's rewarding himself for his progress. Discuss the two situations recorded in his *Coping cat workbook*, focusing particularly on the child's experiences with recalling and using the FEAR plan. Address any difficulties with the four steps. Be encouraging: with practice, the four steps will be almost automatic and not require as much concentration as they do in the beginning.
   - Ask the child to describe his experiences when explaining the 4-step plan to a parent. Reward the child for his cooperation with points, as appropriate. If any part of the STIC was not completed, do it with the child at the start of the session.

2. **Review the idea of progressing from learning to practicing new skills**
   - Remind the child that in today's session he will begin to practice his newly acquired skills in real situations and describe the change in the type of activities that are forthcoming. Instead of learning about the child's thoughts and feelings and learning how to develop coping strategies, the focus will shift to practicing the skills and coping strategies, sometimes in the session/office and sometimes out of the office in the real situation.

3. **Practice using imaginal exposure in low anxiety-provoking situations**
   For each imaginal exposure task practiced:
   - Preparation — FLEX
   Describe the chosen practice situation and discuss/develop a FEAR plan with the child for coping with anxiety (the plan can be entered on p. 44 in the *workbook*). To make the imaginal situation as real as possible, the therapist uses actual items that would be part of the situation as props and asks the child to rate the situation on the 0-8 SUDS scale, or Feelings Thermometer, introduced in Session 2.

➢ Practice [FLEX]

The therapist pretends she is the child and models thinking through the situation out loud while using the FEAR plan to help herself recall the steps to cope. Be a coping model—it doesn't have to be perfect, just a useful illustration. Then the therapist asks the child to think through a slightly different, but similar, scenario using the same props. The therapist may prompt the use of the FEAR plan as needed.

During the imaginal exposure the child provides a SUDS rating before and after the exposure task as well as every minute (or so) during the exposure. The therapist records the child's SUDS rating and rates how anxious she feels the child is, at pre-, during (every minute or so), and post-exposure.

4. **Practice using in-vivo exposure in low anxiety-provoking situations**
For each in-vivo exposure task practiced:
➢ Preparation — [FLEX]

In preparation for the in-vivo exposure task, the therapist and child develop a FEAR plan for coping with the upcoming anxious situation and enter it in the *Coping cat workbook*. The therapist and child negotiate a reward to be given for completing the in-vivo task.

➢ Practice [FLEX]

Using props as appropriate, the therapist asks the child to use his new skills in an actual situation that had been practiced through the imaginal procedure, with the therapist accompanying the child as he carries out the exercise. As this is the first attempt to practice in real life, the therapist asks the child to have available his FEAR card and to check it if he begins to experience difficulty. If the child is not able to proceed at any point in the practice, the therapist encourages self-reward for the partial success he did achieve. She then joins him in the exercise, providing prompts as needed. When the child is successful with the therapist's participation, he is asked to use the steps independently in a similar situation.

Throughout the in-vivo exposure, the child provides a SUDS rating before and after the exposure task as well as every minute during the exposure. The therapist records the child's SUDS rating and also rates how anxious she feels the child is, using the same scale at pre-, during (every minute), and post-exposure (see Kendall et al., 2005a and Session 10's "Tips from the Trenches" for a description of SUDS and the potential uses of SUDS). The child is rewarded for effort and completing the in-vivo.

5. **Briefly review relaxation exercises**

➢ If there is time, a relaxation practice exercise can be done with the child at the close of the session, with a reminder to continue at-home practice with his relaxation CD/tape. Remind the child that relaxation can be used as his first response when becoming anxious, and expand on the idea of a quick relaxation exercise such as a few deep breaths and relaxing the muscles he tends to tighten.

6. **Plan exposure task(s) for Session 11**

➢ Using the situations cards/fear ladder in the *Coping cat workbook* (pp. 74-77), the therapist and child decide on the situation that the child will practice in Session 11. The situation is one that is associated with low levels of anxiety.

7. **Assign STIC task**

➢ Ask the child to review and practice using the FEAR steps in at least one anxious situation, similar to those practiced during the session and to record his experiences in his *workbook*. Negotiate a reward for the out of session in-vivo practice.

➢ The child is also asked to cut out a picture from a magazine or draw a picture of a cartoon character (or sci-fi character) who can help him cope when he is feeling anxious and to bring his character to the next session.

➢ Take a few minutes to play a game or engage in a fun activity at the end of the session as a reward for the child's participation in his first practice session.

Tips from the Trenches

Session 10

The tips for therapists provided to this point have been specific to each treatment session. The following Tips --a longer list-- apply to ALL of the sessions that include exposure tasks (Sessions 10-16). The reader interested in additional information about exposure tasks with children is referred to the discussion and suggestions in an article entitled "Conducting CBT with anxious youth? Think exposures" *Cognitive and Behavioral Practice, 12,* 136-148 (Kendall et al, 2005a).

➤ **Be prepared, and be confident.** That is, know what features of the situation are distressing and have ideas in mind for addressing them. Be encouraging and supportive, and exude confidence: it's amazing how youth will "give it a go" with the right preparation. Your style will influence the child's willingness to be involved. The exposure tasks are never punitive.

➤ When preparing to complete an imaginal or in-vivo exposure task, be sure to ask the child about aspects of the situation that are likely to be troublesome so that the therapist and child can **problem-solve ways to cope with the potential difficulties prior to the exposure task.**

➤ Note for the child how **imagining how to handle a situation (an imaginal exposure task) is helpful for beginning to use various coping strategies.** Practice helps in the actual situation.

➤ If the child is extremely anxious, **the therapist continues with imaginal exposure tasks until the child's level of anxiety is reduced** and the child is able to demonstrate use of the coping plan.

➤ The child's involvement is critical. **Increase involvement by soliciting the child's suggestions** in planning the exposure tasks. The therapist can toss out ideas, but include the child's opinions on how to make the exposure especially useful. The child's suggestions are evidence of involvement and are welcomed.

➤ **The fear hierarchy (situation cards/fear ladder) may need to be changed or amended throughout the exposure sessions** to reflect changes in the level of fear in the child-reported situations. Some degree of adjustment is expected.

However, be cautious not to accept the child's self report (e.g., "Oh, that situation isn't stressful for me any more") that the hierarchy needs to be changed. Instead, test out the situation with the child as an "experiment", in a nonconfrontive fashion.

➤ **Do not be drawn to "protect" the child** from his negative emotions. One of the features of in-vivo exposure is for the therapist to <u>allow</u> the child to become anxious. Any natural tendency to reassure, comfort, "save," or protect the child is held back so the child can begin to develop/display independent skills for coping. Children may try to avoid the in-vivo experience by engaging the therapist in talking excessively about the situation and all its difficulties. The concerns are addressed, but the child, nevertheless, approaches the situation.

➤ Note: **do not "battle" with the child about an exposure task.** If the child is resistant to participate, be patient. Also, the therapist can work with the child to modify the current exposure task a bit or generate an alternative practice situation. Although some negotiation is acceptable, it is important for the therapist not to allow the child to avoid genuine experience with and practicing in the feared situation.

➤ During exposure tasks, the therapist needs to **be aware of "subtle avoidance"** behavior. Subtle avoidance behavior during an exposure task will not allow the child to face the situations "full on." For example, the socially anxious child may be imaging and practicing "going to a school activity," but when he gets to the activity he may stand by himself, not talking to anyone. The preferred experience would include engaging in a conversation. Another example could be the separation anxious child who brings a special object into an anxiety-provoking situation in order to make the situation feel safe (e.g., mother's car keys). Yet another example is the anxious child who uses distraction to think of something completely different when in the anxiety-provoking situation. Although all of these behaviors allow the child to face the situation, in a way the child is prevented from facing the situation full on. It is okay for the child to use a behavior such as these as a coping strategy to begin with (because this is a step by step process), but eventually it is preferred that the child face the situation without any crutches.

➤ **Various in-vivo experiences can be arranged in the office:** setting up testing situations, having the child give a speech or read a poem in front of a small audience, using a video camera to tape the child, and/or having the child introduce himself to other office personnel.

➢ **Many natural-occurring exposure tasks can occur in public places** (e.g., malls, arcades, churches, restaurants, playgrounds, etc.) or in academic and social situations arranged in schools with the help of teachers and guidance counselors. The use of naturally occurring exposure tasks is encouraged because of their less-contrived, true to life nature.

➢ **Other exposure experiences are planned within the office, but carried out with parental help as they naturally occur** (e.g., going to a party or inviting a friend over a child's house). Parental involvement allows the therapist greater flexibility in planning, but this depends on the parents' abilities and motivation. Such situations as family trips, separations, or band/play/sports team tryouts are naturally occurring opportunities that can be used.

➢ **SUDS ratings taken during the exposure situation can have multiple uses:**

   ✦ SUDS ratings can provide feedback to the child about the level of anxiety in the context of the feared object/situation.

   ✦ SUDS ratings can be viewed and treated as "data" regarding what happens to the youth's anxiety when in a specific situation. The child and therapist can graph the data and discuss the SUDS ratings (e.g., Did the anxiety ratings go down at all? Did the ratings go up first before they went down? Do the ratings for each exposure task follow a pattern?).

   ✦ SUDS ratings can be used to determine the exposure task length. To maximize beneficial gains, most exposure tasks call for children to remain in contact with the feared stimulus or in the provocative situation until SUDS are reduced by at least 50 percent.

Practicing in Low Anxiety-Provoking Situations Using Exposure Tasks
Session 11

Purpose

Continue practicing and applying the skills for coping with anxiety in situations that produce low levels of anxiety for the child.

Goals

1. Review STIC task from Session 10
2. Continue practicing using in-vivo exposure in low anxiety-provoking situations
3. Plan exposure task(s) for Session 12
4. Assign STIC task

Tasks

1. ### Review STIC task from Session 10

   ➢ Ask the child to share his picture or cartoon (sci-fi) character drawing who can help him cope with his anxiety.

   ➢ Discuss with the child his anxious experience--the experience he practiced during the week. Reward the child's cooperation with points/stickers as appropriate. If any part of the STIC was not completed, do it with the child at the start of the session or practice the anxious experience planned for the STIC during today's session if possible.

2. ### Continue practicing using in-vivo exposure in low anxiety-provoking situations

   For each in-vivo exposure task practiced:

   ➢ Preparation  F L E X

   Describe the chosen practice situation for the child. To prepare, the therapist and child develop a FEAR plan for coping with the upcoming anxious situation and enter it in the *Coping cat workbook* (p. 49). Anticipate the child's negative thinking and avoidance behavior, and have in place a plan to engage in the situation despite any hesitancy. The therapist and child negotiate a reward to be given after the child completes the in-vivo.

   The therapist then sets up props to create a scene and asks the child to role play the situation as he goes through the FEAR plan. For example, if the task will involve initiating a conversation with a small group of people who are sitting together, then the "props" for the situation, in addition to 3 or 4 colleagues who will role-play being kids in the school cafeteria, include lunch trays, food, and perhaps a lunch bell.

   F L E X

   ➢ Practice

   Ask the child to actually practice the situation that he has role played and to note any difficulties with use of the FEAR steps. The therapist then encourages positive self-rating and self-reward for partial success and helps with any portion of the exercise where the child experienced difficulty. If required, the child repeats the exercise, using the FEAR plan without the therapist's help.

Throughout the in-vivo exposure task, the child provides a SUDS rating every minute and then again at the completion of the practice. The therapist also provides her own SUDS ratings of how anxious she feels the child is at pre-, during (every minute), and post-exposure.

Following the exposure task the child is rewarded. Help the child to make sense of the experience after it is completed: discuss what the child found easiest and most difficult and develop ideas for further improvement.

3. Plan exposure task(s) for Session 12

> Using the situations cards/fear ladder in the *Coping cat workbook* (pp. 74-77), collaborate with the child and decide on the situation that will be practiced in Session 12. The situation is associated with moderate levels of anxiety. Mention that next week the child will be practicing his coping skills using the FEAR plan in more challenging situations and maintain a positive, adventurous outlook.

4. Assign STIC task

> Ask the child to practice using the FEAR steps in two anxious situations that provoke mild anxiety and to record in his *workbook* what happened for discussion during the next session. Collaborate on a reward for the STIC tasks.

Practicing in Moderately Anxiety-Provoking Situations Using Exposure Tasks
Session 12

Purpose

Practice applying the skills for coping with anxiety in imaginal and in-vivo situations that produce moderate levels of anxiety in the child.

Goals

1. Review STIC task from Session 11
2. Practice using imaginal exposure in moderately anxiety-provoking situations
3. Practice using in-vivo exposure in moderately anxiety-provoking situations
4. Plan exposure task(s) for Session 13
5. Assign STIC task

Tasks

1. **Review STIC task from Session 11**

   ➢ Review and discuss the two anxious experiences the child experienced (exposed himself to) during the week. Have him describe how he coped with the anxiety and how he rewarded himself. Reward the child's cooperation with points/stickers as appropriate. If the STIC was not completed, practice the anxious experiences planned for the STIC during today's session if possible.

2. **Practice using imaginal exposure in moderately anxiety-provoking situations**

   For each imaginal exposure task practiced:

   ➢ Preparation  F L E X

   The therapist describes the chosen practice situation that is anticipated to cause moderate levels of anxiety and collaboratively develops a FEAR plan with the child. To make the imaginal situation as real as possible, the therapist uses actual items that would be part of the situation as props and asks the child to rate the situation using the Feelings Thermometer introduced in Session 2.

   ➢ Practice F L E X

   As a coping model, the therapist (acting as the child) models thinking through the situation out loud, using the FEAR plan. Then the therapist asks the child to think through a slightly different, but similar, scenario using the same props, with the therapist prompting the use of the FEAR plan as needed.

   Throughout the imaginal exposure the child provides a SUDS rating before and after the exposure as well as every minute during the exposure. The therapist records the child's SUDS rating and also rates how anxious she feels the child is, using the same scale.

3. **Practice using in-vivo exposure in a moderately anxiety-provoking situation**

For each in-vivo exposure task practiced:

➤ Preparation ⟵ F L E X

In preparation for the in-vivo exposure task, the therapist and child develop a FEAR plan for coping with the upcoming anxious situation (the plan can be entered on p. 53 in the *workbook*), thinking through what might and might not happen and preparing for the several more likely aspects of the event. The therapist and child negotiate a reward to be given if the child completes the in-vivo.

➤ Practice F L E X

The therapist and child leave the office and go to a location in which the child can practice, in real life, the situation of moderate anxiety he has just role played/imagined. For example, gathering information (a survey) that requires talking to new people, purchasing something from a local store and being short a few cents, etc. Transportation, if necessary, is arranged prior to the session.

To present a coping model, the therapist remarks on aspects of the situation that might be generating anxiety in the child. Covering each point in the FEAR plan, the therapist describes her thoughts and leaves open the opportunity for the child to comment on the situation or provide suggestions to help the therapist cope better. Importantly, in this out-of-the-office exposure task, the child collaborates with and helps the therapist use the steps of the FEAR plan.

The child is asked to describe his own feelings, somatic reactions, and anxious self-talk, as well as how to be adaptive. The therapist and child discuss appropriate coping strategies and reserve several minutes to do a relaxation exercise before and/or in the actual situation. Be sure to help the child develop actual strategies for coping within the situation and "think through" how to carry them out. If more than one aspect of the situation is troubling to the child, the therapist may want to address the different aspects separately.

Throughout the in-vivo exposure task, the child provides a SUDS rating before and after the exposure as well as every minute along the way. The therapist records the child's SUDS rating and also rates how anxious she feels the child is, using the same scale at pre-, during (every minute), and post-exposure.

Following the exposure task, the child is rewarded for effort/completing the in-vivo exposure task. The therapist and child discuss what the child found easiest and most difficult and develop ideas for further improvement.

4. **Plan exposure task(s) for Session 13**
   ➤ Using the situations cards/fear ladder in the *Coping cat workbook* (pp. 74-77), the therapist and child decide on the situation that the child will practice in Session 13. The situation that is selected is associated with moderate levels of anxiety.

5. **Assign STIC task**
   ➤ Ask the child to practice using the FEAR steps in at least two anxious situations that provoke moderate levels of anxiety and to record what happened for discussion during the next session. Negotiate a reward for each out of session practice.
   ➤ Using the coping character the child cut out or created as part of the STIC for Session 10, the child is asked to make up a story about how that character could help other children cope in a situation like one that might make him feel anxious.
   ➤ Remind the child that there are only four more sessions!

Practicing in Moderately Anxiety-Provoking Situations Using Exposure Tasks
Session 13

Purpose

Practice applying the skills for coping with anxiety in real (in-vivo) situations that produce moderate levels of anxiety in the child.

Goals

1. Review STIC task from Session 12
2. Practice using in-vivo exposure in moderately anxiety-provoking situations
3. Plan exposure task(s) for Session 14
4. Assign STIC task

Tasks

1. **Review STIC task from Session 12**

   ➤ Discuss the two anxious experiences the child faced during the week. Have him describe how he coped with the anxiety, even if it went only partially well, and how he rewarded himself.

   ➤ Ask the child to share the story about his cartoon character who found himself in a scary situation. Discuss how successful the character coped with his fears and worries. Reward the child's cooperation with points or stickers as appropriate. If part of the STIC was not completed, complete the story and/or practice the anxious experiences planned for the STIC during today's session if possible.

2. **Practice using in-vivo exposure in moderately anxiety-provoking situations**

   For each in-vivo exposure task practiced:

   ➤ Preparation ◁ F L E X

   Discuss the anxious situation that was selected in Session 12 to practice in today's session. To prepare, the therapist and child develop a FEAR plan for coping with the upcoming anxious situation (the plan can be entered on p. 58 in the *workbook*), Think it though, processing with the child the experience that they are about to enter. Negotiate a reward to be given to the child for effort/completion of the task.

   ➤ Practice

   The therapist and child leave the office and go to a location in which the child can practice using the FEAR steps, in real life, the situation of moderate anxiety he has just discussed with the therapist. Transportation, if necessary, is arranged prior to the session.

   To present a coping model, the therapist remarks on aspects of the situation that might be generating anxiety and covers each point in the FEAR plan.

The child is asked to describe his own feelings, somatic reactions, and anxious self-talk, as well as how to better manage anxious arousal. The therapist and child discuss appropriate coping strategies and reserve a few minutes to do a relaxation exercise before and/or in the actual situation. Be sure to help the child develop actual strategies for coping within the situation and think through how to carry them out. Again, if more than one aspect of the situation is troubling to the child, the therapist addresses the different aspects separately.

As done in previous exposure tasks, the child provides a SUDS rating before and after the exposure as well as every minute during the exposure. The therapist records the child's SUDS rating and also provides a rating.

Following the exposure task the therapist guides an evaluation of the child's performance, discussing what the child found easiest and most difficult. Help the child note even partial success on any or all parts of the FEAR plan. Ideas are developed for further improvement and the child is rewarded for effort/completing the in-vivo exposure task.

3. **Plan exposure task(s) for Session 14**

    ➤ Using the situations cards/fear ladder in the *Coping cat workbook* (pp. 74-77), the therapist and child decide on the situation that the child will face in Session 14. The situation is associated with high levels of anxiety. Mention to the child that next week he will be using his coping skills in a more challenging situation—maintain and encourage a positive, adventurous outlook.

4. **Assign STIC task**

    ➤ Remind the child to practice using the FEAR steps in at least two anxious situations that provoke moderate levels of anxiety and to record what happened for discussion during the next session. Arrange a reward for the child's efforts.

    ➤ Remind the child that there are only three more sessions!

Practicing in High Anxiety-Provoking Situations Using Exposure Tasks
Session 14

Purpose

Practice applying the skills for coping with anxiety in imaginal and in-vivo situations that produce high levels of anxiety in the child.

Goals

1. Review STIC task from Session 13
2. Practice using imaginal exposure in high anxiety-provoking situations
3. Practice using in-vivo exposure in high anxiety-provoking situations
4. Plan exposure task(s) for Session 15
5. Assign STIC task

Tasks

1. ### <u>Review STIC task from Session 13</u>

    ➢ Discuss with the child the two anxious experiences he practiced during the week. Have him describe how he coped with the anxiety and how he rewarded himself. Reward the child's cooperation and effort with points or stickers as appropriate. If the STIC was not completed during the past week, practice the anxious experiences planned for the STIC during today's session if possible.

2. ### <u>Practice using imaginal exposure in high anxiety-provoking situations</u>

    Note that at this point in treatment, many children will be able to apply the FEAR plan without assistance. Nevertheless, because the situation will be challenging, the therapist has to maintain enthusiasm and a supportive environment. Use the following imaginal procedures as needed for increasingly stressful situations.

    For each imaginal exposure task practiced:

    ➢ Preparation — FLEX

    Describe the chosen practice situation that will cause high levels of anxiety and collaborate on a FEAR plan for coping (the plan can be entered on p. 61 in the *workbook*). To make the imaginal situation as real as possible, use props that would be part of the situation. Have the child rate the situation with the Feelings Thermometer introduced in Session 2.

    ➢ Practice FLEX

    Use the props to help create the situation of high anxiety and encourage the child to describe the scenario that he can then role play with minimal assistance from the therapist. Again, be careful to ensure that the child includes modification of his anxious self-talk and a coping plan. In addition, the therapist may find that in the more stressful situations, the child has a greater number of fears and worries that have to be addressed in his coping plans.

70

Throughout the imaginal exposure the child provides a SUDS rating before and after the exposure as well as every minute during the exposure. The therapist records the child's SUDS rating and also rates how anxious she feels the child is, using the same scale at pre-, during (every minute), and post-exposure.

3. **Practice using in-vivo exposure in high anxiety-provoking situations**

For each in-vivo exposure task practiced:

➢ Preparation ← FLEX

In preparation for the in-vivo exposure task, the therapist and child collaborate to develop a FEAR plan for coping with the upcoming situation. The therapist and child negotiate/arrange a reward for effort and cooperation.

➢ Practice FLEX

The therapist and child leave the office and go to a location in which the child can practice, in real life, the situation of high anxiety he has just role played/imagined. Transportation, if necessary, is arranged prior to the session.

To present a coping model, the therapist remarks on aspects of the situation that might be generating anxiety. Cover each point in the FEAR plan, and self-disclose related self-talk. Encourage the child to comment on the situation and to provide suggestions to help the therapist cope better. Importantly, the child (now himself an expert) helps the therapist use the steps of the FEAR plan.

The child is asked to describe his own feelings, somatic reactions, and anxious self-talk. Be sure to include the child describing how to make his self-talk more adaptive. Discuss appropriate coping strategies and reserve a few minutes to do a relaxation exercise before and/or in the actual situation. Be sure to help the child develop actual strategies for coping within the situation and discuss/role play how to carry them out. Again, if more than one aspect of the situation is likely to be troubling to the child, address the different aspects separately.

Throughout the in-vivo exposure, the child provides a SUDS rating before and after the exposure as well as every minute during the exposure. The therapist records the child's SUDS rating and also rates how anxious she feels the child is, using the same scale at pre-, during (every minute), and post-exposure.

Following the exposure tasks, the child is rewarded for effort and completion. Collaborate and discuss what the child found easiest and most difficult and develop ideas for further improvement.

4. **Plan exposure task(s) for Session 15**
   ➢ Using the situations cards/fear ladder in the *Coping cat workbook* (pp. 74-77), decide on the stressful situation(s) that the child will practice in Session 15.

5. **Assign STIC task**
   ➢ Ask the child to practice using the FEAR steps in at least two anxious situations that provoke high levels of anxiety and to record what happened for discussion during the next session. Negotiate a reward for each out of session in-vivo practice.
   ➢ Introduced as a fun opportunity, the child is asked to start thinking about a "commercial" that he can produce in the final session (Session 16). For example, he can show other people how to cope with a scary situation. If the child prefers, he can feature his cartoon character. The commercial can be designed for radio, TV, or newspapers, or can be a poem, song, brochure, booklet, skit, or anything else that the child would like to do. Encourage creativity!
   ➢ Remind the child that there are only two more sessions!

Tips from the Trenches
Session 14

> The end of treatment commercial provides an opportunity for success in a creative task and a demonstration of success in managing anxiety. **How the child completes the commercial is very flexible.** It is in the child's words, at the child's level, and fun. Examples of the end of treatment commercial include rap songs, skits, poems, puppets, stories, drawings, websites, and cartoons that are both informative and humorous. Videotape the commercial, give it a professional-looking label, and refer to it as documentation of (recognition of) the child's accomplishments. Children can be given a copy of their product to take home as a concrete accomplishment.

Practicing in High Anxiety-Provoking Situations Using Exposure Tasks
Session 15

Purpose

Practice applying the skills for coping with anxiety in in-vivo situations that produce high levels of anxiety in the child.

Goals

1. Review STIC task from Session 14
2. Practice using in-vivo exposure in high anxiety-provoking situations
3. Plan a closing exposure task for Session 16
4. Discuss briefly the end of treatment
5. Assign STIC task

Tasks

1. **Review STIC task from Session 14**

   ➤ Discuss with the child the anxious experiences during the past week, noting the different fears and worries that the child noticed in the situations. Have him focus on and describe how he coped with the anxiety and how he rewarded himself. If the STIC was not completed during the past week, practice the anxious experiences planned for the STIC during today's session if possible.

   ➤ Have the child share his ideas for the commercial. If there was little **FLEX** preparation, do the brainstorming and planning in the session. Talk with him about the characters and any props or scenery that will be needed for the commercial and make specific plans for filming the commercial. Provide the child with the option of filming the commercial at home (versus in session), if the child's family owns a camcorder. Making the tape with the therapist is preferred, but if the child decides to film the commercial at home, be sure the child brings in the videotape so that it can be viewed during the last session. Reward the child as appropriate.

2. **Practice using in-vivo exposure in high anxiety-provoking situations**

   For each in-vivo exposure task practiced:

   ➤ Preparation —— **FLEX**

   Discuss the anxious situation selected in Session 14 to practice in today's session. In preparation for the in-vivo exposure task, develop a FEAR plan for coping with the anxious situation and record it in the *Coping cat workbook* on p. 67. Arrange a reward for the child.

   ➤ Practice

   The therapist and child leave the office and go to a location in which the child can practice using the FEAR steps, in real life, in the situation of high anxiety he has just discussed with the therapist. Transportation, if necessary, is arranged prior to the session.

As a coping model, the therapist remarks on aspects of the situation that might be generating anxiety. Carefully covering each point in the FEAR plan, the therapist describes her thoughts and encourages the child to comment on the situation or provide suggestions to help the therapist cope better. Importantly, the child helps the therapist use the steps of the FEAR plan.

The child is asked to describe his own feelings, somatic reactions, and anxious self-talk, as well as how to make it more adaptive. The therapist and child discuss appropriate coping strategies and reserve several minutes to do a relaxation exercise before and/or in the actual situation. Help the child develop actual strategies for coping within the situation and discuss how to carry them out. Again, if several aspects of the situation are troubling to the child, address the different aspects separately.

SUDS ratings provide information to review with the child. Have the child provide SUDS ratings before, during and after the exposure task. The therapist records the child's SUDS rating, and also rates how anxious she feels the child is, using the same scale at pre-, during (every minute), and post-exposure.

Following the exposure task (after each exposure task when there are more than one), the therapist helps to evaluate the child's performance, discussing what the child found easiest and most difficult. Help the child to note successes on the parts of the FEAR plan and not just to focus on the final result when he evaluates his work. Ideas are developed for further improvement and the child is rewarded. Keep in mind, rewards are highly varied (individualized for the child). It may be easiest to give a small toy, but pointing out to the child naturally occurring rewards (e.g., getting to play with a friend is a reward for inviting a friend over) and social rewards (e.g., social activities, games, or a walk outside) is preferable.

3. **Plan a closing exposure task for Session 16**

   ➤ The next session will be the last session for practicing the FEAR plan in anxious situations. Using the situations cards/fear ladder (pp. 74-77 of the *Coping cat workbook)*, collaborate with the child to select a challenging (and probably successful) situation for Session 16. The situation is associated with high levels of anxiety, but also keep in mind that ending on a positive experience is preferred.

4. **Discuss briefly the end of treatment**

   ➤ Remind the child that the next session is the last one. Briefly recap what the child has accomplished and learned, emphasizing his progress during the previous weeks. Convey confidence in the child's ability to maintain his treatment gains with continued practice at home. Encourage the child to share his feedback about the treatment process and ask him to share any questions or concerns that he may have about terminating treatment. Inform the child that you will be asking his parents to join the last session so that you can review his progress and say goodbye.

5. **Assign STIC task**

   ➤ Ask the child to use the FEAR steps in two anxious situations and to record what happened for brief discussion during the last session. Negotiate a reward for each out of session in-vivo practice.

   ➤ The next session is the last session and will involve videotaping of the brief (a few minutes) commercial. Prepare any materials that will be needed to complete the task. As you prepare for the last session and the commercial, keep in mind that it should be fun—it's a chance for the child to "show off" and celebrate his successes. If the child anticipates doing the commercial at home, think it through with him and remind him to bring in the videotape so that it can be viewed during the session and the proper enthusiasm can be engendered. After the session, if parents have been cooperative, encourage them to help the child prepare the commercial and make arrangements to attend the next session.

Tips from the Trenches

Session 15

➤ **Address the facts that (a) therapy will be ending and (b) the relationship with the therapist will no longer be on a regular schedule.** This transition can be difficult for some clients. Children may begin to talk about increased anxiety and physical symptoms during the final weeks of treatment, almost suggesting a want for the session to continue. Informing the child at the end of each session (beginning at Session 12) how many sessions are left helps the child understand that his time with you is coming to an end. Encourage the child to talk about the end of therapy and help the child envision possible feelings that might occur during the last weeks or after the end of therapy. Applying the FEAR plan to this situation (e.g., worrying about how things will be without the therapist) is also suggested when the child shows signs of distress associated with terminating treatment.

➤ As the therapist, keep in mind that it is important to **provide ample support for the child in the belief that he is now ready to do well without the therapist.** Not perfect, but better. It is often a good idea to discuss possible upcoming difficult situations and how the child might handle these difficulties using the FEAR plan.

Practicing in High Anxiety Situations, Producing the Commercial, and Terminating Treatment
Session 16

Purpose

Provide a final practice task applying the skills in an in-vivo exposure that produces high levels of anxiety in the child. Produce the "commercial." Review and summarize the training program. Make plans with the parents to help the child maintain and generalize newly acquired skills. Bring closure to the therapeutic relationship.

Goals

1. Review STIC task from Session 15
2. Conduct a final exposure task in a high anxiety-provoking situation
3. Have fun producing the "commercial"
4. Review and summarize the treatment program and bring closure to the therapeutic relationship

Tasks

1. ### Review STIC task from Session 15

   ➤ Review the anxious experiences the child was exposed to during the week, focusing on his autonomous efforts, his progress to date, and any special ways he has been able to become less anxious. As he describes how he coped with the anxiety and how he rewarded himself it can be helpful to applaud the improvements and share pride in the gains. At this juncture, the child is likely doing things that he could not do at the start of treatment. Reward the child appropriately. If the STIC was not completed during the past week, practice the anxious experiences planned for the STIC during today's session if possible.

2. ### Conduct a final exposure task in a high anxiety-provoking situation

   For each in-vivo exposure task practiced:

   ➤ Preparation  F L E X

   Discuss the anxious situation selected in Session 15 to practice in today's session. Create a FEAR plan for coping with the anxious situation and enter it on p. 70 of the *workbook.* Keep in mind that we want this to be a successful experience for the child.

   ➤ Practice   F L E X

   The therapist and child leave the office and go to a location in which the child can practice the situation just discussed using the FEAR plan, in real life. Transportation, if necessary, is arranged prior to the session. Because this is the final session, the exposure task is conducted at a nearby location so as to reserve time for the production of the commercial, a discussion of treatment termination, and some fun.

   As in past exposure tasks, the therapist can remark on aspects of the situation that might be generating anxiety in the child. However, it is good to have the child do this for himself. The child can describe his own feelings, somatic reactions, and anxious self-talk, as well as how to make it more adaptive. If the child wants to just "do it" and is moving forward (approaching) into the situation without distress, this can be supported. Importantly, the child is transitioned to take more of the lead in the use the steps of the FEAR plan.

As in the past exposure tasks, gather SUDS ratings.

Following the final exposure task, think through and talk about the child's performance—note the progress since the start of treatment. Help the child note success on any or all parts of the FEAR plan.

3. **Have fun producing the "commercial"**

   ➢ Prior to the session, the therapist prepares the room where the taping will take place. If additional people are needed, make necessary arrangements. A blank tape/CD and videotaping equipment are prepared, and some materials to decoratively label the video are available.

   ➢ Review, with some guidance but without grand expectations, the final arrangements for filming. Integrate the materials that the child has prepared for the filming to those already set up. Have fun with a practice run (or dress rehearsal).

   ➢ Videotape the brief commercial and view it. It is often that parents are invited to view the tape, and sometimes parents are included in making the tape. The content and quality of the video is less important than the celebratory context of the event: the child has come along way and there is a recognition and reward for this progress. Parents may need to be guided to see the advances and not to harp on imperfections. Make a copy of the tape so that both the child and the therapist have one.

4. **Summarize the treatment program and bring closure to the relationship**

   ➢ Recap with the parents and child what has been accomplished over the course of treatment. Review with the parents the "FEAR" acronym, ceding the expert role to the child. Note that there have been gains but that there are areas still in need of improvement—this is always the case.

➤ Encourage the parents to share their feedback about their child's progress and ask any questions or share any concerns that they may have about concluding treatment.

➤ Describe for the parents (as was done with the child) that there may be times that are difficult in terms of coping with anxiety--this is normal. But, with continued practice there comes continued improvement. Given the expertise of the therapist, share any specific recommendations. These may include new ways for the parents to behave around their child (granting the child more autonomy) or situations in need of continued practicing. If necessary, offer referrals for additional services (e.g., an obese child may want to try to loose weight). The parents and child are given the therapist's card and are invited to call if they have any further questions/concerns, but they are also told to call to inform the therapist as to how the child is progressing. In short, the therapist invites further contact around future successes.

➤ Inform the parents that you will call to "check-in" and see how the child is doing. If appropriate, schedule a meeting for a posttreatment assessment and ask the parents to bring their current contact information for follow-up.

➤ When the parents seem comfortable and satisfied with the discussion, ask them to leave for a few minutes so that you can share a "good-bye" with the child. When the parents have left the office, express your satisfaction with and encouragement for the child's efforts and present the child with a certificate (last page of the *Coping cat workbook*) to commemorate completion of the treatment program. Have the certificate cosigned by an official (give the certificate added meaning, and provide an opportunity for another person to congratulate the child). During these moments, share some of the highlights of the therapy experience and ask the child to do the same. Begin to create the "history" of the treatment by talking about what has transpired. Encourage the child to continue to use what has worked for him and convey confidence in his ability to do so successfully. At the same time, point out that it is reasonable for there to be new situations and future times that may seem challenging. Remind the child that you will call in four weeks to talk about how he's doing.

FLEX

Tips from the Trenches
Session 16

> During the last session, **provide the child with a final reward for participation** in the program. It is suggested that the reward be a social reward, such as playing a favorite game with the therapist, having a pizza "party" with the parents and therapist, going out for ice cream, or sharing some other activity. The time is set aside for having fun and the focus is kept on present and future accomplishments. The session may run longer than usual.

> The **therapist discusses with the child's parents how to support what has been learned** and to encourage use of the FEAR steps and willingness to try new tasks.

Therapist Resources
Comorbidity and Complicating Factors

It is difficult to imagine any child whose problems are so circumscribed that they fit only the basic DSM or ICD criteria for a diagnosis of an anxiety disorder. Rather, many children who meet one set of diagnostic criteria often present with a variety of other symptoms as well (e.g., depression/dysthymia, hyperactivity, obsessions/compulsions, panic attacks).

In addition to problems of comorbidity, children may experience other complicating factors (e.g., realistic fears, family difficulties) and/or show behavior more directly connected to their primary anxiety disorder that could potentially interfere with treatment (e.g., hypercriticism, denial of anxiety, over-compliance and noncompliance, and school refusal. These instances require special attention.

Considered in this section are the special needs linked with various types of comorbidity and other complicating factors that may potentially impact treatment.

Comorbidity

➢ Depression/Dysthymia

The overlap between anxiety and depression is recognized (Brady & Kendall, 1992; Kendall, Brady, & Verduin, 2001; Kendall & Watson, 1989). Anxiety and depression share a number of symptoms, including irritability, agitation/restlessness, concentration difficulties, insomnia, and fatigue. Given this overlap, it is not surprising that a number of studies have revealed a high correlation between self-report measures of anxiety and depression (see Gotlib & Cane, 1989; Brady & Kendall, 1992). However, whereas there is a strong indication for the comorbidity of depression and anxiety in both children and adults (Saylor, Finch, Spirito, & Bennett, 1984), the degree to which they overlap remains in dispute.

One might expect that a number of children seeking treatment for anxiety problems may also be experiencing some depressive symptoms. It is the recognition of the possibility that prompts us to use a measure of depressive symptoms in our assessment: to be alert to depressive symptoms from the start of treatment. In the course of considering the ways this treatment program can be modified to address depression, it is worthwhile to consider some of the similarities and differences, particularly at the emotional and cognitive level, which have been posited between depression and anxiety (see Kendall, Kortlander, Chansky & Brady, 1992).

Regarding differences at the emotional level, fear has been posited as a central component of anxiety whereas sadness has been considered central to depression (Izard, 1971). In addition, anxiety and depression have been differentiated along dimensions of the global constructs, negative and positive affect (Watson & Clark,

1984). Anxiety has been characterized as a state of negative affect (e.g., not excited, enthusiastic, or joyful; see Kendall & Watson, 1989). These findings suggest that while an anxious (but not depressed) child may experience a number of negative emotions, he/she may still have a relatively strong capacity for joy. On the other hand, a child who is both anxious and depressed may carry the double burden of experiencing a number of negative emotions with less hope of any relief offered by intermittent enjoyment.

The presence of depression has implications for the treatment of anxiety. First, because a cognitive-behavioral program involves a number of assignments that are done outside of the session, therapists may face a situation in which the dysphoric child's low motivation interferes with finishing these tasks. If the child is feeling hopeless, he may not see the value of completing the STIC assignments. The therapist moves the client along, offers the hope that she believes the child will feel less sad, and that completing the assigned task is one important step for feeling better. To sustain an atmosphere of hopefulness, the therapist is particularly encouraging about any attempts that are made to complete the tasks. Parents are an important resource (not interfering with the child and potentially encouraging the child throughout the week to complete the assignments). It is important that parents not be overbearing and inadvertently critical of their children's work. It is the case that some parents of children with anxiety problems have been overtly critical and judgmental, and this is also the case for dysphoric and depressed children. Helping parents to become supportive and encouraging, without "hovering," facilitates treatment progress.

Within each session, the therapist will want to emphasize "fun" activities; anxious children who are also dysthymic may have developed the habit of assuming they aren't going to have fun, so why try. For example, by engaging in various games (e.g., computer games or traditional board games) the child may be surprised that he is capable of engaging in a pleasurable activity. If deemed reasonable, the therapist may encourage parents to provide opportunities for fun at home.

Recognizing that he is capable of enjoying activities is tied to the child's implementing the fourth and final step in our "FEAR" acronym—Reward. With an increasing capacity for pleasure, the child will become more ready to think of ways of rewarding himself. Helping the dysphoric child discover means of self-reward is an important intervention in and of itself. Parents can be involved by pointing out times at home when the child can reward him/herself, as depressed and anxious children tend to focus on their mistakes and faults rather than accomplishments.

Working with an anxious child who is also somewhat depressed may entail addressing certain ongoing cognitive activities that are less likely to be found in a purely anxious child. Anxious children who are also depressed have cognition associated with anxiety as well as typically depressogenic cognition: the more depressed cognition includes a greater emphasis on personal degradation and a greater preoccupation with the past. Because depressogenic attributions often involve focusing on past behavior as well as self-degradation for performance in past situations, depressive cognition can be addressed at the "E" (expectations), "A" (actions and attitudes), or "R" (results and rewards) step of the FEAR plan. In evaluating their performance in anxious situations, depressed children would be expected to make more internal attributions about negative outcomes than anxious children who are not depressed (see Kendall, Stark & Adam, 1990). By exploring these expectations and attributions for performance, therapists can help children become more aware and start to modify their dysfunctional thinking. Again, the therapist can involve the parents in addressing the child's depression. The therapist helps the parent to point out that feelings of depression are not permanent.

Conducting personal experiments, as used in treating depressed youth (see Lewinsohn & Clarke, 1999; Stark et al., 2006), resembles the collaborative empiricism of Beck's cognitive-behavioral therapy for depression (Beck, Rush, Shaw, & Emery, 1979; Hollon & Beck, 1979). In these "tests", clients are asked to describe situations and report their attributional conclusions. A shared experience with the therapist allows both the child and therapist to have some reasons for certain attributions, and the therapist can help the child think of ways to test such notions. For example, if the child and therapist have a shared interaction with another youth and the client thinks that the other child did not like him, the therapist would be able to ask "What made you think that?" and, possibly, "Is there any other way to explain it?" After related discussions and perhaps even further testing of such notions in which the child asks the other person if he liked or disliked him, the therapist and child work together to develop attributional patterns that are more consistent with the data and less biased by the depressed client's views about himself. To facilitate lasting cognitive change in the anxious and dysphoric child, the therapist can reward the child and tie the new causal attributions that have been generated into the "R" step of the FEAR program. The interested reader is referred to *Taking ACTION: A workbook for overcoming depression* (Stark, Kendall, McCarthy, Stafford, Barron, & Thomeer, 1996).

> ## Hyperactivity

Although anxious children may exhibit signs of motor agitation (e.g., hair twisting, stuttering, wanting to leave an anxious situation; Barrios & Hartmann, 1997), hyperactive children are characterized by more impulsiveness (acting without thinking) in situations that require careful thinking (Kendall & Braswell, 1993). In treating an anxious child who may also exhibit some signs of overactivity, the therapist can adjust both cognitive and behavioral parts of the current treatment program. At the behavioral level, the therapist may want to create a more structured approach to teaching the skills that are introduced during the first half of the program. Children with difficulties staying focused on task benefit from structured environments. It is also the case that children receiving this program for anxiety may concurrently be receiving medications other services for ADHD (e.g., Hinshaw, 2006).

Also, anxious-overactive children may find it difficult to learn to relax. For instance, because it may be anxiety provoking for these children to do muscle relaxation (see Heide & Borkovec, 1983; 1984 for a discussion of relaxation-induced anxiety), the skills might be introduced more gradually, with structure, and in terms of a game in which the child is told that he is learning to be a ragdoll. The therapist can move around the room with the child telling him when to make various parts of his body like a ragdoll (i.e., relaxed) and when to make them like a robot (i.e., tensed). In this manner the therapist can participate as a coping model who also learns that it is safe to become relaxed. Family members can serve as coping models as well. It may also be helpful to oversee some of the STIC tasks—have the child draw pictures of anxiety-provoking situations in sessions or right after the sessions before he/she goes home, thus modeling and providing structure. This effort would be intended to prepare the child for the more concentration-demanding task of writing about anxiety producing situations in his *Coping cat workbook*. With a hyperactive child, parents may need to be more involved in overseeing STIC tasks at home, by imposing structure or simply reminding the child.

Other aspects of the current treatment program lend themselves to working with children whose anxiety problems include some hyperactive patterns. A portion of this program involves the therapist's planning and modeling coping procedures. Repeated exposure to anxiety-related situations and "stopping to think" about how to cope with them may help the child reduce impulsivity and cope with anxiety. Overactive children have low levels of frustration tolerance and benefit from learning how to deal with failure without becoming excessively frustrated. We have often found it useful to model coping with making mistakes when working with anxious children who tend to see any error as indicative of personal failure. For instance, the therapist may intentionally fumble with audio equipment (when taping a session) and model a coping style of self-talk, in addition to modeling how to cope with the frustration of making a mistake. Again, parents and older siblings can also be coping models, disclosing mistakes or failure experiences and how they coped. This additional element of potential frustration in the face of making a mistake is added at the "E" of the FEAR steps as one of several cognitive facets in the situation that may be anxiety or frustration producing.

➤ Obsessive-Compulsive Patterns

Obsessional ruminations and compulsive ritualistic behavior has been seen as reflecting distressing levels of anxiety. There are children whose anxiety includes certain obsessive features (Henin & Kendall, 1997) and children who actually receive a diagnosis of obsessive compulsive disorder (Rapoport, 1986).

Because it is often thought that obsession and/or compulsions are anxiety-reducing for the sufferer, the child with such patterns may be highly resistant to changing them. The child may be quite rigid, hypervigilant, and even hostile about protecting this anxiety-reducing behavior because of a vague overwhelming fear of some disaster or harm befalling him. Individuals with obsessive compulsive disorder may not trust their feelings and perceptions about situations, and there is a strong tendency to avoid experiencing emotions if they are going to feel bad or out of control. The preferred way of treating obsessive compulsive disorder emphasizes exposing the individual to the anxiety-provoking situation without allowing the obsessive compulsive pattern to take place (response prevention). The individual is exposed to his/her anxiety at high levels. The FEAR plan can be applied to anxious situations that entail the obsessive compulsive behavior by creating exposure experiences (with response prevention) to address the obsessive compulsive difficulties. The therapist directs the parents in implementing response prevention strategies at home.

The severity of obsessive compulsive patterns varies greatly among the children. One distinction to keep in mind when deciding how to address such patterns is whether or not the pattern seems to represent a budding obsessive compulsive disorder or is rather a less severe byproduct of the perfectionism characteristic of perhaps an associated anxiety disorder (see Comer, Kendall, Franklin, Hudson, & Pimentel, 2004 for a discussion of the overlapping characteristics of obsessive compulsive patterns and generalized anxiety in children). To illustrate these possibilities, consider two examples of anxiety disordered children who have been treated in our clinic. In the case of a girl, we'll call Maggie, the therapist noticed that she was extremely perfectionistic. Overly concerned with making any type of error, she had difficulty completing the self-report forms in a timely fashion because she needed to check each page several times to make sure she had answered every question and queried any item for which she was not absolutely sure that the answer she gave was precise. In the second case, a client, we will call Sara, demonstrated a more extreme obsessive compulsive behavior pattern that interfered with her life. She was preoccupied with not being interrupted and, therefore, spoke very rapidly fearing that any break in her speech would result in an interruption.

Because Maggie's behavior appeared to be directly related to her overall perfectionism, rather than being a compulsion to check her answers, the problem was addressed within the framework of our program for youth with generalized anxiety. The therapist chose to set up an exposure task requiring the child to complete a detailed task within certain time limits that would preclude excessive checking. In presenting the task, the therapist helped the child work through the FEAR steps so that she could cope with the anxiety that would arise in the face of possibly making an error that she did not have time to correct. Such experience, especially when repeated in various forms, helped the child to learn to be less perfectionistic, a common problem in generalized anxiety disorder.

For Sara, a more behavioral intervention, with somewhat less concern about use of the FEAR steps, seemed appropriate. Thus, the therapist asked Sara to engage in a conversation with someone who was instructed to interrupt her. It was anticipated that initially the child's anxiety would mount, but repeated experience with the situation would lead to extinction of the anxiety, and a concurrent reduction in the compulsion to speak very rapidly. Although our efforts did produce modest improvements, Sara did not complete the treatment program.

Because children with obsessive patterns are already extremely caught up in their own cognitive activity, attempts at cognitive exploration of the problem may backfire—leading to an escalation of their tendency to do too much thinking. A child whose overriding problem is obsessional thinking requires caution before undertaking a "heady" program. However, for a child whose primary problem is generalized anxiety with mild obsessive and/or compulsive features, the goal would be to reduce obsessive and/or compulsive patterns so that the anxiety that is related to the generalized anxiety can be fully addressed. When OCD is the primary problem, other systematic approaches should be considered (see Piacentini, March & Franklin, 2006).

➢ Panic Attacks

The child who experiences panic-like symptoms shows extreme concern for physiological responses associated with anxiety. There are a few children with a primary diagnosis of an anxiety disorder who also report panic-like symptoms such as a racing heart, shaking, chattering teeth, and dizziness. Additionally, ill-defined feelings of being overwhelmed have also been reported. Nelles and Barlow (1988) suggested that although children may manifest the physiological signs of panic, it is debatable whether prior to adolescence children are cognitively capable of making the internal attributions for their symptoms that are necessary for the cognitive component of panic attacks (e.g. "I'm going to die" [pg. 369]). Nelles and Barlow note that the incidence of diagnosed panic disorder in children is extremely low.

Despite the low incidence of childhood panic attacks, it is worthwhile to consider how the *Coping cat* program might be used to address these associated symptoms, even if they do not constitute a full panic attack. Because the panic-like symptoms can themselves be anxiety-provoking, it is appropriate to address them within the FEAR plan so that the child can learn to cope with such distressing physiological arousal. Such an approach entails helping the child identify what the initial physiological cues are that may spark the fear of experiencing intense physiological arousal. Having learned what responses typically foreshadow this arousal, a child can proceed to cope via the first of the FEAR steps—Feeling Frightened? For instance, a child reports that a suddenly-racing heartbeat is his typical response before the general escalation of other physiological responses, and he learns to use this response as a cue to ask himself if he is feeling frightened. However, in the case of panic-like symptoms, the question would be used to identify whether the child was feeling frightened about the heart beat because it signaled the possibility of panic-like symptoms, or because of fear of some external circumstance. The child would then use the recently-acquired skills to "calm down;" while taking deep breaths often works to initially calm anxiety, they may in the case of nascent panicky symptoms, exacerbate hyperventilation which has been associated with the onset of panic (Ley, 1987). Thus, the child might want to focus on relaxing tense muscles instead.

Should the child's level of cognitive development permit, he might be encouraged to use the next step—"Expecting bad things to happen?" The child would be encouraged to focus on panic-related cognition: Is he expecting to lose control or is he fearing that he might be overwhelmed by the physiological symptoms and actually die? The goal of the first steps would be to nip in the bud the mounting physiological symptoms and the distorted thinking about these symptoms before the full-blown panic-like experience ensues. Because the escalation of physiological symptoms may be extremely rapid and intense, making the child aware of distorted thinking may be especially difficult; the therapist will have to be prepared to be particularly persistent in probing about this information. In the "Actions and Attitudes" step of the FEAR plan, the child can be encouraged to think of various ways to cope other than merely escaping from the arousing situation (such action readily reinforces avoidance behavior). Coping may involve the use of relaxation not only to prevent the anxiety but also to lower anxiety if it has begun to escalate (see Barlow & Cerny, 1988, for a cognitive-behavioral treatment of panic in adults). Coping may also include coping self-talk: "I know how to breathe; my body knows what to do".

The therapist may want to assess the parents' responses to the child's panicky symptoms. Parents may exacerbate the situation by being overreactive to the child's distress and by not allowing the child to cope independently. The family could role play an enactment of what happens when the child has a panicky reaction so that the therapist can notice how family members respond. The therapist can offer suggestions to parents about how they can handle the situation and they can role play this new behavior. If a parent is overreactive, the parent is encouraged to employ strategies to contain his/her own distress so that he/she can better help the child. Parents are directed to help the child implement his own coping strategies from the FEAR steps.

Other Complicating Factors

> **Problems with Compliance**

Anxious children are often concerned about pleasing others, and, in some instances, become overcompliant. Indeed, one of the reasons that anxious children often go without treatment is, unlike children with more externalizing symptoms (e.g., conduct disorder), anxious children's symptoms often result in compliance with others. The signs of overcompliance may include completing all STIC assignments perfectly as well as dutifully just going through the motions, afraid to question any assignments or express when he or she does not understand. The child may become anxious if he believes he has not done something exactly as it was supposed to have been done. One way to address this is for the therapist to encourage an instance of "noncompliance." For example, an overly compliant child (in fact, many of the clients) can be told that he must choose not to complete one of the STIC tasks (homework assignments). This slight deviation from doing what is expected may be very anxiety provoking. Yet, such a situation provides an opportunity for helping the overly-compliant child learn how to cope with anxiety when he misconstrues that something was done "wrong."

Though anxious children are often eager to please, occasionally children are reluctant to comply with the various activities involved in cognitive-behavioral treatment. Noncompliance can range from an out-right failure to complete the STIC tasks to passivity within the sessions. In trying to handle noncompliance, the therapist may want to ask what the behavior represents—what is the catastrophe that the child has thought of? For instance, a child may report that he is bored in the sessions and simply does not believe that there is very much in need of attention. However, such behavior may reflect a real fear of discussing very upsetting thoughts and feelings. A very intelligent 13-year-old girl, for example, felt ashamed that she was terrified whenever one of her parents was 15 minutes late after work. She had great difficulty opening up and telling the therapist that she imagined her parent to be dead.

Great patience and a willingness to try different approaches are needed in dealing with the noncompliant anxious child. Acknowledging that the child doesn't seem interested in what is being discussed, and following with probes about the reasons for this disinterest can be helpful. Asking the child how things might be better for him in the sessions, or an open recognition of some of the child's nonanxious emotions, such as anger or depression, are other possibilities. Extra efforts at rapport building may be required, such as finding a favorite activity (e.g., computer games) and using it during the session while at the same time accomplishing the session tasks. The goal is to strike a balance between making the noncompliant child aware that you empathize with the difficulty of discussing problems (and even their feelings that nothing is going to help), while at the same time projecting confidence that if they are willing to participate more thoroughly they really will be able to help themselves in difficult and painful situations.

➢ Hypercriticism

When working with an anxious child who is hypercritical the therapist can encourage and reward less-than-perfect performance on many STIC as well as in-session tasks. For instance, highly perfectionistic children fear doing anything that appears "sloppy." One little girl became upset when she accidentally got a pencil mark on a piece of paper on which she was about to draw. She immediately wanted to get a fresh sheet. The therapist asked her to use the original sheet and to use the FEAR steps to cope with appearing sloppy. The therapist explored the child's worries and fears—what might happen if she does something less than perfectly—particularly in reference to how they think others will perceive them. Hypercriticism can be addressed at the results and reward stage of the FEAR steps. These children find it very difficult to realistically assess their performance, seeing anything less than perfect as failure. One of the aims of the program is to help children realize that they do not have to perform perfectly in order to feel they have succeeded, and this point receives special emphasis when working with a hypercritical child.

Some parents of anxious children are hypercritical towards their own behavior or to that of the child. Thus, the parent's hypercriticism is a model for the child and reinforces the child's hypercriticism. The therapist can ask the parent to model recognition of their hypercritical behavior, and help them to more accurately assess their own performance. The parent can also model self-reward as it is not uncommon for the parent to have difficulty with this idea too. It is essential that the therapist help the parents to have realistic expectations of the child. The therapist can help the parents to modify the demands for perfect or overachieving behavior in their child.

➢ Denial of Anxiety

Anxious children may exhibit behavior that can interfere with treatment. This behavior is often related to their presenting problems. Among the most common is the initial denial of anxiety. For instance, consider the following: One of the instruments used to assess anxiety in children is a self-report questionnaire that asks the client how frequently he has difficulty making up his mind. The child is seated at a table and is reading and rereading the item. The alternatives are read and reread, and the therapist is approached with a question about the item. Even after the therapist has provided clarification, the child continues to labor over the item and "shows" genuine difficulty making up his mind. Eventually, after much consternation, the child reports that he does not have difficulty making up his mind. Thus, the questionnaire data (self-report) seems in contradiction to the observed actions. While it is only speculation, it seems that the child wants to present in a favorable manner (fake good) and has misinterpreted his own difficulties in making decisions to avoid reporting anxiety (see Kendall & Chansky, 1991).

More generally, it is not unusual for a child to be somewhat willing to report some anxious feelings during a diagnostic intake interview, only to report during an initial therapy session that he has no real problems with anxiety. More than likely, such denial represents the child's attempt to appear competent in the eyes of the therapist. It can be very helpful at such times for the therapist to disclose her own feelings of anxiety in certain situations. In addition, having family members disclose anxiety may also encourage the child to be more open. Such an approach normalizes the experience and can relieve the anxious child of the need to try to appear perfect and competent.

Sometimes, children actually exhibit several signs of anxiety (e.g., extreme hair twisting, nervous giggling, nervous motor activity) and yet when questioned whether they are feeling anxious, report no anxious feelings. This situation can be dealt with in several ways. The therapist may draw attention to the behavior and question; "I notice you're twisting your hair, I twist my hair when I'm nervous, do you?" It may be helpful again for the therapist to self-disclose as a coping model—showing how it can be easy to say you aren't anxious when you really are. This modeling can include statements about how it is difficult to get help coping with anxious feelings if people don't let anybody know how they are feeling. Another strategy is to have each family member report about a situation that makes another family member anxious. This exercise may help to normalize anxiety as each family member is described in an anxious situation. Having someone else report about a time the child was anxious may in this context allow the child to acknowledge at least some anxiety.

➢ School Refusal

Given the nature of school refusal, often families and/or schools are very desperate for solutions to the disruptions associated with the avoidance of school. The timing of the interventions, based on when the child's skills are in place and when the involved parties are ready to cooperate, is an important decision for the therapist. Attempting an intervention too soon can be detrimental (e.g., having the child attend school after an extended absence without first consulting the school staff). Similarly, a failure situation may be used by parents as evidence that the situation is unalterable and that other measures are needed (e.g., making the child switch to another school).

Specificity is often the key to success, thus the following guidelines are in the service of identifying the specific instances (contingencies) where school attendance difficulties arise, how they are currently being handled, and what strategies have been attempted unsuccessfully in the past.

Working with school avoidant children

If a child is missing school due to avoidance, then implementation of a plan to keep the child in school must start early in treatment. Often separation anxiety and anxiety about particular situations at school co-occur, thus both problems need to be addressed in the treatment.

Children may be surprised, if not overwhelmed with all the attention the school avoidance has been receiving from angry teachers and parents alike. Therefore, while the therapist will be asking the child about school and other separation situations during Sessions 2-3 when discussing stressful situations, it is important that *other* low-stress situations be discussed as well. Conveying empathy for the child's situation is always important, but particularly when the child may be receiving negative, angry messages from adults in his life.

Early sessions involve learning about the types of school difficulties the child is having. Questions to consider include: Does the child have friends? Are there children teasing him? Is there a particular teacher of whom the child feels afraid? Does the child feel behind in any particular class due to absences? In general how is he feeling about his ability to keep up in school? How does the child cope with structured time (class time) versus unstructured time (recess, lunch, playing before school)?

Assessing strengths and resources is equally important. Is there a teacher or counselor at school with whom the child feels particularly safe? Are the child's friends in the same class? Are there some favorite activities which might be used as a reward for the child's courage and cooperation?

Importantly, once a plan has been established for the child to return to school, specific strategies need to be developed with the child. For example, if the child is feeling upset in the morning or on the walk to school or during class, what can he do? A child survival pack of stickers, helpful positive thoughts, or strategies (e.g., making eye contact with a friend) can be brought to school as tangible reminders of the child's coping mechanisms. A reward such as making contact with a favorite teacher or counselor at the end of the day is arranged. Depending on the age of the child, the parents can be told of the child's own plan so that they may help the child to remember to use it. If the child cries, has outbursts, or in some way disrupts the classroom, an additional option may be to have a room or space away from the class where the child can sit quietly for a few minutes to collect himself. This "pause" can include contact with a teacher or counselor, but should be firmly time-limited and geared toward the next step of getting back to class (See teacher interventions below).

Working with parents of school avoidant youth

The first step when working with parents of school avoidant youth is to learn more about how the school avoidance has developed and exactly how it has been handled in the past. This will include exploration of any difficulties at home which may be of concern to the child (e.g., abuse, alcoholism). A non-threatening question can be asked to assess this: "Though we are a child-focused treatment, we need to be aware of any situations in the child's life which may be worrying him or interfering with his day-to-day activities—whether this be in the home (any illnesses or conflict) or in the neighborhood (crime)." After assessing any potential "parent" problems, the therapist discusses how these problems might interfere with the child treatment, and discuss options (e.g., referring the parents for treatment) to address these problems.

General information-gathering includes answers to such questions as "How long has this problem been going on?" "In what ways does it interfere in the child's life?" "When does the child first start to protest school (night before, morning of)?" "How does the child protest—crying, stomachaches, temper tantrums?" "Which parent typically responds and how?" "How does the parent get the child to school?" "When does the parent "concede" the fight, i.e., when do you let the child stay home?" "How do parents work together or against each other?" "How does each think the situation should be handled?" Answers to these questions help the therapist be proactive in developing a plan that will prevent possible failure. For example, a plan will be undermined if a parent is unable to bear hearing their child say "My stomach is coming apart and I'm gonna die," and knowing this allows the therapist to help the parent plan to cope with the distress. The therapist supports the parent in how difficult it can be is to hear their child upset, but offers direction—hug the child and say you are sorry the child is not feeling well but that it's time to go to school.

Discuss parents' fears. The therapist may need to discuss parent fears at length, until parents are clearly reassured that making their child go to school is both developmentally appropriate (they're not asking their child to do anything that other children their age could not do) and a positive parental responsibility. The parents are advised that the transition may be difficult for them, but that their child does want to grow up and go to school. Set the expectation that upset, crying, and hurt feelings may be part of the process and that they should not be afraid of the initial distress: reassure parents that their children will know that they still love them—and that the children need their help in solving this problem. The therapist conveys her belief that this problem is manageable and that success is imminent as long as everyone keeps to the plan.

Sometimes a written agreement is provided for parents. The written information describes how to get the child to school—verbal encouragements, supportive statements, and firm directions to get the child ready for school and for being dropped off at school (or at the bus). For example, if a child is yelling (or crying) at home in the morning, the parents have the written suggestions to acknowledge the distress, give verbal support, but continue to help the child get dressed or get breakfast, etc.

Shaping can be used. It may be worthwhile during the first few days of the plan to drop the child off immediately prior to the start of class rather than 15 minutes prior to school. The unstructured time before class begins may be too difficult for the child to manage. During the second or third week if the child is ready, earlier arrival can be incorporated.

The "R" of the FEAR plan (Results and rewards) is central to success. Explain the value of "reward" to the parents, how it helps increase desired behavior and makes the child feel proud. Rewarding can be fun—parent and child making a chart and choosing rewards. Each day the child earns credit (sticker, points) for going to school, with the expectation that the child will attend school each of the five days and get the preferred reward. With the help of the therapist, parents are encouraged to praise the child when school is attended and the points are awarded and, if the child does not go to school, to refrain from assigning points, but do not punish the child or draw attention to the situation. For example, parents are specifically told and given opportunity to practice not taunting the child: "See, you didn't get any star today, you're not going to get your reward." If the child doesn't go to school, the parents do not assign the points, phone the therapist and discuss what went wrong, and make a plan for how to get back on track.

Arrangements for the reward are made in advance. Often parents are reluctant to reward their children for something that the parents think they should do for nothing. Parents may feel resentful, "I never got a reward for going to school." These concerns must be addressed, otherwise parents may undermine the reward and thus the overall plan. Have parents somewhat involved in the selection of the reward—in other words, within their price range or time constraints. Explain to parents that the return to school is challenging and scary for their child and although they will not be required forever, rewards will help solve the problem at this time. Also, assure them that once the child is back at school, the rewards will be faded out. It is worth noting that, often, separation anxious children are happy with non-monetary rewards such as spending special time with parents.

Working with the school personnel of school avoidant youth

Working with school avoidant youth benefits from coordinated efforts with teachers, counselors, and school principals. Begin with information gathering from key individuals (e.g., teacher or counselor) and find out what other school personnel may be involved in the school avoidance. This may include the school nurse, for example, who sends the child home from school when he complains of stomachaches. Maintain a stance that is cooperative and supportive. Find out how the avoidance has been problematic for the school and learn what resources the school has. For example, a teacher may know of a "buddy" to link the child up with to help the child feel comfortable in school, or may have access to rewards for the child.

Useful questions for the school personnel include: "What is the school's stance about the problem?" "How long has the problem been going on?" "Does the child have difficulty 1st thing in the morning?" "After certain classes?" "How has the school been handling the problem?" (find out the exact contingencies). "Is the child spending time in the nurse's office or the counselor's office?" "Is the child sent home often?" "What is a reasonable system for managing the child's distress?" "Is there a place where the child can go for 2-3 minutes to collect himself before returning to the classroom?"

➤ Realistic Fears

Therapists need to be sensitive to the reality basis of a child's distress. Children from low SES groups have been found to have more fears about specific events or things—perhaps resulting from the reality that their environments contain more threatening events. Such first hand experiences with very threatening situations, situations that children in other circumstances would simply never have to face, can result in detrimental anxiety. For example, one of our adolescent clients had a fear of being stabbed; as it turned out she had actually been stabbed and had seen others being stabbed during various street fights. Stressful and threatening environments contributing to the child's anxiety are not limited to children from low SES backgrounds. Children from various SES groups may live in chaotic homes where there is a relative lack of parental support because the parents themselves are under great stress (e.g., from work, marital problems, being a single parent, or illness).

At a pragmatic level, a disorganized home environment may create difficulties for treatment effectiveness in terms of lost relaxation tapes, notebooks, or other session related materials. Likewise the child may have trouble completing schoolwork, which in turn may contribute to his anxiety about school performance. On an emotional level, parents who are under stress may at times be somewhat unpredictable. Thus, for example, one 12-year-old boy suffered a great deal of anxiety about being hurt by bigger children. In somewhat ambiguous situations, such as being bumped in the hall at school during the crowded rush to classes, he would perceive the other children as trying to harm him. The origins of these fears became clearer when, during the parent session, the mother reported that the father, who was currently working two jobs, was presently very moody and unpredictable in his behavior toward the child, at times lashing out and hitting him for only minor transgressions. Similarly, if a parent is him/herself experiencing extreme anxiety and presenting the world as a threatening place to the child, the child's fear may be grounded in the fear-filled "reality" that is presented by the parent. The therapist needs to be sensitive to the parent's anxiety, but the focus of treatment is on helping the child learn to recognize realistic fears and stressful circumstances and to identify strategies to cope with them. An integral part of this involves helping the child learn to distinguish between what are reality-based fears and what fears and worries result from misinterpretation or over generalization of situations which are similar to fearful situations that the child actually faces (e.g., the threat of an unpredictable father versus being bumped in the school hall).

> **Family Difficulties**

The present program is geared toward helping the child to cope with his anxiety. The problems described so far have been problems that children might bring into treatment. Although we have mentioned ways parents might contribute to or maintain the child's difficulty and how they can be encouraged to help the child, parents and other family members also may create difficulties to the therapeutic process.

One of the goals of the program is to consider family factors that may be maintaining the child's difficulties. Common problems may include parents who are overly critical or overprotective, and inappropriate limit setting. These factors will be addressed as part of the therapy process. However, in some cases, children will be learning the FEAR steps, but the parents will not be receptive to the therapist's input regarding changes they need to make. To encourage receptiveness on the part of parents, therapists need to take care that parents do not feel unduly blamed or criticized. Their strengths as parents need to be emphasized as well as their potential weaknesses.

In some cases, parents may try to monopolize time to discuss their own problems that are not directly relevant to the child's anxiety. Though the therapist needs to be compassionate, the therapist also needs to keep the therapy on track and goal oriented and redirect the parents to the task at hand. For example, if a parent is overly identified with the child and constantly talks about his/her own anxiety, this information can be incorporated into the exposure sessions, the therapist would emphasize the distinction between the parent's feelings and the child's. In other cases, parents or siblings will bring up completely unrelated material such as work problems. If necessary, the therapist may spend a portion of separate time with the parents to address issues and consider making outside referrals for the parents.

Parental psychopathology, substance abuse, or marital problems all may negatively impact on the therapy process because the parents may be less motivated, or less able to change behavior that contributes to or maintains the child's difficulty. In any of these instances, the therapist tries to capitalize on strengths in the family or ways that one or more family members can compensate for problems.

If a parent is depressed, for example, the parent may have difficulty following through on out-of-session suggestions. A parent's depression may serve to reinforce a negative attributional style in the child through modeling, and may diminish positive reinforcement of the child by the parent. Depression may also contribute to marital difficulties, and marital conflict can have a negative effect on the child as well.

If there are marital problems, one parent may be less invested in helping the child overcome anxiety. It is not uncommon to find that when a separation anxious child sleeps in the parent's bed, marital problems help to maintain the behavior. The therapist has to encourage the parents to work together in helping the child. However, at times, if one parent has serious psychological problems which contribute to a difficult relationship with the child, encouraging the other parent to become more involved with the child may lessen the stress in the family as long as this involvement does not cause the child-parent alliance to be stronger than the marital alliance.

If a parent tends to lash out at the child when the parent is stressed, the therapist can help the family to identify the warning signs and have them use the FEAR plan to think of different ways to handle the situation. The child's role play may include a parent who acts out different ways on handling a stressful situation, with the therapist's help. The plan may simply involve recognition of the warning signals and the parent and child going to different parts of the house until the parent cools off. The parent may be able to use relaxation exercises to calm him/herself.

Substance abuse on the part of a parent can also create difficulties in treatment. In some cases, the family will keep the substance abuse hidden, and the therapist may sense that there is a secret. In such cases, it may be easier for the parents to reveal this problem in a separate meeting with the therapist.

Closing Comments

Although this manual allows for the flexibility needed to deal with children who have a variety of problems, the primary and principal focus is on helping children learn how to manage and cope with distressing anxiety. Thus, in assessing whether or not a child's problems are amenable to treatment within a cognitive-behavioral framework, one must consider how much the child's general functioning will be helped if he learns to cope more successfully with anxiety. In making such a decision, it may be helpful to conceptualize potential difficulties in treatment as lying along a continuum, ranging from symptoms of anxiety to the presence of other disorders. Some problems, such as hypercriticism or overcompliance, may be products of the child's fundamental anxiety. Other problems, such as comorbid depression, obsessive compulsive patterns, or hyperactivity, involve a more complex situation that may relate to functional difficulties outside the realm of anxiety. In general, the degree to which the program will likely be useful for children displaying symptoms of other disorders and for children in families with significant problems besides the child's anxiety will vary with the individual child and his family and the skill of the therapist. Our goal associated with the previous suggestions is to help determine how best to approach potential difficulties in treatment and help facilitate flexible applications of a structured intervention. Therapist supervision provides opportunities for discussing these and other potential difficulties. It is urged that therapists have access to supportive and encouraging supervision on a regular basis.

References

Barlow, D., & Cerny, J. (1988). *Psychological treatment of panic*. New York: Guilford Press.

Barrett P., Dadds, M., & Rapee, R. (1996). Family treatment of childhood anxiety: A controlled trial. *Journal of Consulting and Clinical Psychology, 64,* 336-342.

Barrios, B., & Hartmann, D. (1997). Fears and anxieties. In E. Mash and L. Terdal (Eds.). *Assessment of childhood disorders* (3rd ed., pp. 196-264) New York: Guilford.

Beck, A. T., Rush, A., Shaw, B., & Emery, G. (1979). *Cognitive therapy of depression.* New York: Guilford Press.

Brady, E., & Kendall, P. C. (1992). Comorbidity of anxiety and depression in children and adolescents. *Psychological Bulletin, 111,* 244-255.

Chambless, D., & Hollon, S. (1998). Defining empirically supported treatments. *Journal of Consulting and Clinical Psychology, 66,* 5-17.

Chansky, T. E., & Kendall, P. C. (1997). Social expectations and self-perceptions of children with anxiety disorders. *Journal of Anxiety Disorders, 11,* 347-365.

The Child Anxiety Network (2001). *I Can Relax! Relaxation CD for Children.* http://childanxiety.net/.

Chu, B.C. & Kendall, P.C. (2004). Positive association of child involvement and treatment outcome within a manual-based cognitive-behavioral treatment for anxious youth. *Journal of Consulting and Clinical Psychology, 72,* 821-829.

Comer, J., Kendall, P.C., Franklin, M., Hudson, J. & Pimentel, S. (2004). Obsessing/worrying about the overlap between obsessive-compulsive disorder and generalized anxiety disorder in youth. *Clinical Psychology Review, 24,* 663-683.

Creed, T.A. & Kendall, P.C. (2005). Empirically supported therapist relationship-building behavior within a cognitive–behavioral treatment for anxiety in youth. *Journal of Consulting and Clinical Psychology.*

Fauber, R., & Kendall, P. C. (1992). Children and families: Integrating the focus of interventions. *Journal of Psychotherapy Integration, 2,* 107-124.

Flannery-Schroeder, E., & Kendall, P. C. (1996). *Cognitive behavioral therapy for anxious children: Therapist manual for group treatment.* Ardmore, PA: Workbook Publishing.

Gotlib, I., & Cane, D. (1989). Self-report assessment of depression and anxiety. In P. C. Kendall & D. Watson (Eds.), *Anxiety and depression: Distinctive and overlapping features* (pp. 131-169). New York: Academic Press.

Heide, F., & Borkovec, T. (1983). Relaxation-induced anxiety: Paradoxical anxiety enhancement due to relaxation training. *Journal of Consulting and Clinical Psychology, 51,* 171-182.

Heide, F., & Borkovec, T. (1984). Relaxation-induced anxiety: Mechanisms and theoretical implications. *Behavior Research and Therapy, 22,* 1-12.

Henin, A., & Kendall, P. C. (1997). Obsessive compulsive disorder in children and adolescents. In T. H. Ollendick & R. J. Prinz (Eds.) *Advances in clinical child psychopathology* (vol. 19, pp. 75-131). New York: Plenum Press.

Hinshaw, S. (2006). Attention-deficit/hyperactivity disorder. In P. C. Kendall (Ed.) (3rd edition), *Child and adolescent therapy: Cognitive-behavioral procedures.* New York: Guilford Press.

Hollon, S., & Beck, A. T. (1979). Cognitive therapy of depression. In P.C. Kendall & S. Hollon (Eds.), *Cognitive-behavioral interventions: Theory, research, and procedures* (pp. 153-203). New York: Academic Press.

Howard, B., Chu, B.C., Krain, A., Marrs-Garcia, A., & Kendall, P.C. (2000). *Cognitive-behavioral family therapy for anxious children: Therapist manual.* Ardmore, PA: Workbook Publishing.

Howard, B., & Kendall, P. C. (1996). Cognitive-behavioral family therapy for anxiety-disordered children: A multiple-baseline evaluation. *Cognitive Therapy and Research, 20,* 423-444.

Hudson, J., Krain, A., & Kendall, P. C. (2001). Expanding horizons: Adapting manual-based treatments for anxious children with comorbid diagnoses, *Cognitive and Behavioral Practice, 8,* 338-346.

Izard, C. (1971). *The face of emotion.* New York: Appleton-Century-Crofts.

Kazdin, A. E., & Weisz, J. (1998). Identifying and developing empirically supported child and adolescent treatments. *Journal of Consulting and Clinical Psychology, 66,* 19-36.

Kendall, P. C. (2006). Guiding theory. In P. C. Kendall (Ed.), *Child and adolescent therapy: Cognitive-behavioral procedures* (3rd ed.). New York: Guilford.

Kendall, P.C. (2000). *The Coping cat workbook.* Ardmore, PA: Workbook Publishing.

Kendall, P. C. (1993). Cognitive-behavioral therapies with youth: Guiding theory, current status, and emerging developments. *Journal of Consulting and Clinical Psychology, 61,* 235-247.

Kendall, P. C. (1994). Treating anxiety disorders in youth: Results of a randomized clinical trial. *Journal of Consulting and Clinical Psychology, 62,* 100-110.

Kendall, P. C., Brady, E. U., & Verduin, T. L. (2001). Comorbidity in childhood anxiety disorders and treatment outcome. *Journal of the American Academy of Child and Adolescent Psychiatry, 40,* 787-794.

Kendall, P. C., & Braswell, L. (1993). *Cognitive-behavioral therapy for impulsive children (2nd ed.).* New York: Guilford Press.

Kendall, P. C., & Chansky, T. E. (1991). Considering cognition in anxiety-disordered children. *Journal of Anxiety Disorders, 5,* 167-186.

Kendall, P.C., Choudhury, M.A., Hudson, J., & Webb, A. (2002). The C.A.T. Project Manual. Ardmore, PA: Workbook Publishing.

Kendall, P. C., Chu, B., Gifford, A., Hayes, C., & Nauta, M. (1999). Breathing life into a manual: flexibility and creativity with manual-based treatments. *Cognitive and Behavioral Practice, 5,* 177-198.

Kendall, P. C., Flannery-Schroeder, E., Panichelli-Mindel, S., Southam-Gerow, M., Henin, A., & Warman, M. (1997). Therapy for youths with anxiety disorders: A second randomized clinical trial. *Journal of Consulting and Clinical Psychology, 65,* 366-380.

Kendall, P.C., & Hedtke, K.A. (2006). *The Coping cat workbook (2nd edition).* Ardmore, PA: Workbook Publishing.

Kendall, P. C. & Holmbeck, G. (1991). Psychotherapeutic interventions for adolescents. In R. Lerner, A. Peterson, & J. Brooks-Gunn (Eds.), *The encyclopedia of adolescence* (pp. 866-874). New York: Garland Publishing.

Kendall, P.C., Hudson, J., Choudhury, M., Webb, A. & Pimentel, S. (2005b). Cognitive-behavioral treatment for childhood anxiety disorders. In E. D. Hibbs & P. S. Jensen (Eds.) *Psychosocial treatments for child and adolescent disorders: Empirically based strategies for private practice* (pp. 47-74). Washington, DC: American Psychological Association.

Kendall, P. C., Kortlander, E., Chansky, T. E., & Brady, E. U. (1992). Comorbidity of anxiety and depression in youth: Treatment implications. *Journal of Consulting and Clinical Psychology, 60,* 869-880.

Kendall, P. C. & Macdonald, J. P. (1993). Cognition in the psychopathology of youth, and implications for treatment. In K. S. Dobson and P. C. Kendall (Eds.), *Psychopathology and cognition* (pp. 387-427). San Diego: Academic Press.

Kendall, P.C., Robin, J.A., Hedtke, K.A., Gosch, E., Flannery-Schroeder, E., & Suveg, C. (2005a). Conducting CBT with anxious youth? Think exposures. *Cognitive and Behavioral Practice, 12,* 136-148.

Kendall, P.C., Safford, S., Flannery-Schroeder, E., & Webb, A. (2004). Child anxiety treatment: Outcomes in adolescence and impact on substance use and depression at 7.4-year follow-up. *Journal of Consulting and Clinical Psychology, 72,* 276-287.

Kendall, P. C., & Southham-Gerow, M. A. (1995). Issues in the transportability of treatment: The case of anxiety disorders in youths. *Journal of Consulting and Clinical Psychology, 63,* 702-708.

Kendall, P. C., & Southam-Gerow, M. A. (1996). Long-term follow-up of a cognitive-behavioral therapy for anxiety-disordered youth. *Journal of Consulting and Clinical Psychology, 64,* 724-730.

Kendall, P. C., Stark, K. D., & Adam, T. (1990). Cognitive deficit or cognitive distortion in childhood depression. *Journal of Abnormal Child Psychology, 18,* 255-270.

Kendall, P. C., & Treadwell, K. R. H. (1996). Cognitive-behavioral treatment for childhood anxiety disorders. In P. S. Jensen & E. D. Hibbs (Eds.), *Psychosocial treatment research with children and adolescents* (pp. 23-42). Washington, DC: APA.

Kendall, P. C., & Warman, M. J. (1996). Anxiety disorders in youth: Diagnostic consistency across DSM-III-R and DSM-IV. *Journal of Anxiety Disorders, 10,* 453-463.

Kendall, P. C., & Watson, D. (Eds.). (1989). *Anxiety and depression: Distinctive and overlapping features.* NY: Academic.

Koeppen, A. S. (1974). Relaxation training for children. *Elementary School Guidance and Counseling, 9,* 14-21.

Kortlander, E., Kendall, P. C., & Panichelli-Mindel, S. (1997). Maternal expectations and attributions about coping in anxious children. *Journal of Anxiety Disorders, 11,* 297-315.

Krain, A., Hudson, J., Coles, M. & Kendall, P. C. (2002). The case of Molly L: Use of family cognitive-behavioral treatment for childhood anxiety. *Clinical Case Studies, 1,* 271-298.

Lewinsohn, P. M., & Clarke, G. (1999). Psychosocial treatments for adolescent depression. *Clinical Psychology Review, 19,* 329-342.

Ley, R. (1987). Panic disorder. In L. Michelson & M. Ascher (eds.) *Anxiety and stress disorders: Cognitive-behavioral assessment and treatment.* New York: Guilford Press.

Nelles, W., & Barlow, D. (1988). Do children panic? *Clinical Psychology Review, 8,* 359-372.

Ollendick, T. H., & Cerny, J. A. (1981). *Clinical behavior therapy with children.* New York: Plenum Press.

Ollendick, T. H., & King, N. (1998). Empirically supported treatments for children with phobic and anxiety disorders. *Journal of Clinical Child Psychology, 27,* 156-167.

Ollendick, T. H., King, N., & Chorpita, B. (2006). Empirically-supported treatments for children. In P. C. Kendall (Ed.) (3rd edition), *Child and adolescent therapy: Cognitive-behavioral procedures.* New York: Guilford Press.

Piacentini, J., March, J., Franklin, M. (2006). Cognitive-behavioral therapy for youngsters with obsessive-compulsive disorder. In P. C. Kendall (Ed.) (3rd edition), *Child and adolescent therapy: Cognitive-behavioral procedures.* New York: Guilford Press.

Rapoport, J. (1986). Childhood obsessive compulsive disorder. *Journal of Child Psychology and Psychiatry, 27,* 289-295.

Ronan, K., Kendall, P. C., & Rowe, M. (1994). Negative affectivity in children: Development and validation of a self-statement questionnaire. *Cognitive Therapy and Research, 18,* 509-528.

Saylor, C., Finch, A., Spirito, A., & Bennett, B. (1984). The Children's Depression Inventory: A systematic evaluation of psychometric properties. *Journal of Consulting and Clinical Psychology, 52,* 955-967.

Southam-Gerow, M., & Kendall, P. C. (2000). A preliminary study of the emotion understanding in youth referred for treatment of anxiety disorders. *Journal of Clinical Child Psychology, 29,* 319-327.

Stark, K., Hargrave, J., Sander, J., Custer, G., Schnoebelen, S., Simpson, J., & Molnar, J. (2006). Treatment of childhood depression: The ACTION treatment program. In P. C. Kendall (Ed.) (3rd edition), *Child and adolescent therapy: Cognitive-behavioral procedures.* New York: Guilford Press.

Stark, K., Kendall, P. C., McCarthy, M., Stafford, M., Barron, R., & Thomeer, M. (1996). *Taking ACTION: A workbook for overcoming depression.* Ardmore, Pa: Workbook Publishing.

Suveg, C., Comer, J., Furr, J., & Kendall, P. C. (2006). Adapting manualized CBT for a cognitively-delayed child with multiple anxiety disorders. *Clinical Case Studies.*

Treadwell, K. R. H., & Kendall, P. C. (1996). Self-talk in anxiety-disordered youth: States-of-mind, content specificity, and treatment outcome. *Journal of Consulting and Clinical Psychology, 64,* 941-950.

Treadwell, K. R. H., Flannery, E. C., & Kendall, P. C. (1995). Ethnicity and gender in relation to adaptive functioning, diagnostic status, and treatment outcome in children from an anxiety clinic. *Journal of Anxiety Disorders, 9,* 373-384.

Watson, D., & Clark, L. (1984). Negative affectivity: The disposition to experience negative emotional states. *Psychological Bulletin, 96,* 465-490.

ISBN-13: 978-1-888805-22-2
ISBN-10: 1-888805-22-6